FRANCIS FRITH'S

LANCASHIRE VILLAGES

BORN AND BRED in Lancashire, Catherine Rothwell has been associated with local history for forty years. Daughter of a professional photographer and a Fellow of the Library Association, before retirement she was Deputy Borough Librarian of Fleetwood, and was later in charge of all reference and local history books for Lancashire Library in the Borough of Wyre. Her sixty published books reveal an in-depth knowledge of Lancashire and above all, the intrinsic spirit of a valiant shire rich in tradition. Catherine lives in Poulton-le-Fylde, and has three children and four grandchildren

FRANCIS FRITH'S
PHOTOGRAPHIC MEMORIES

LANCASHIRE
VILLAGES

PHOTOGRAPHIC MEMORIES

CATHERINE
ROTHWELL

First published in the United Kingdom in 2003 by
Frith Book Company Ltd

Paperback Edition 2003
ISBN 1-85937-496-4

British Library Cataloguing in Publication Data

Francis Frith's Lancashire Villages
Catherine Rothwell

09270765

Frith Book Company Ltd
Frith's Barn, Teffont,
Salisbury, Wiltshire SP3 5QP
Tel: +44 (0) 1722 716 376
Email: info@francisfrith.co.uk
www.francisfrith.co.uk

Printed and bound in Great Britain

Front Cover: **GRINDLETON**, *the Village 1899* 43494

Frontispiece: **CHATBURN**, *c1950* C462007

CONTENTS

FRANCIS FRITH: VICTORIAN PIONEER   7

LANCASHIRE VILLAGES - AN INTRODUCTION   10

THE PENDLE WITCHES TRAIL   16

UP HILL AND DOWN DALE   30

BRIDGES, CHURCHES AND OTHER TOUCHSTONES   58

THATCHED COTTAGES AND THE SEA   84

INDEX   115

Free Mounted Print Voucher   *119*

FRANCIS FRITH
VICTORIAN PIONEER

FRANCIS FRITH, founder of the world-famous photographic archive, was a complex and multi-talented man. A devout Quaker and a highly successful Victorian businessman, he was philosophic by nature and pioneering in outlook.

By 1855 he had already established a wholesale grocery business in Liverpool, and sold it for the astonishing sum of £200,000, which is the equivalent today of over £15,000,000. Now a multi-millionaire, he was able to indulge his passion for travel. As a child he had pored over travel books written by early explorers, and his fancy and imagination had been stirred by family holidays to the sublime mountain regions of Wales and Scotland. 'What a land of spirit-stirring and enriching scenes and places!' he had written. He was to return to these scenes of grandeur in later years to 'recapture the thousands of vivid and tender memories', but with a different purpose. Now in his thirties, and captivated by the new science of photography, Frith set out on a series of pioneering journeys up the Nile and to the

Near East that occupied him from 1856 until 1860.

INTRIGUE AND EXPLORATION

These far-flung journeys were packed with intrigue and adventure. In his life story, written when he was sixty-three, Frith tells of being held captive by bandits, and of fighting 'an awful midnight battle to the very point of surrender with a deadly pack of hungry, wild dogs'. Wearing flowing Arab costume, Frith arrived at Akaba by camel seventy years before Lawrence of Arabia, where he encountered 'desert princes and rival sheikhs, blazing with jewel-hilted swords'.

He was the first photographer to venture beyond the sixth cataract of the Nile. Africa was still the mysterious 'Dark Continent', and Stanley and Livingstone's historic meeting was a decade into the future. The conditions for picture taking confound belief. He laboured for hours in his wicker dark-room in the sweltering heat of the desert, while the volatile chemicals fizzed dangerously in their trays. Back in London he exhibited his photographs and was 'rapturously cheered' by members of the Royal Society. His reputation as a photographer was made overnight.

VENTURE OF A LIFE-TIME

Characteristically, Frith quickly spotted the opportunity to create a new business as a specialist publisher of photographs. He lived in an era of immense and sometimes violent change.

For the poor in the early part of Victoria's reign work was exhausting and the hours long, and people had precious little free time to enjoy themselves. Most had no transport other than a cart or gig at their disposal, and rarely travelled far beyond the boundaries of their own town or village. However, by the 1870s the railways had threaded their way across the country, and Bank Holidays and half-day Saturdays had been made obligatory by Act of Parliament. All of a sudden the working man and his family were able to enjoy days out and see a little more of the world.

With typical business acumen, Francis Frith foresaw that these new tourists would enjoy having souvenirs to commemorate their days out. In 1860 he married Mary Ann Rosling and set out on a new career: his aim was to photograph every city, town and village in Britain. For the next thirty years he travelled the country by train and by pony and trap, producing fine photographs of seaside resorts and beauty spots that were keenly bought by millions of Victorians. These prints were painstakingly pasted into family albums and pored over during the dark nights of winter, rekindling precious memories of summer excursions.

THE RISE OF FRITH & CO

Frith's studio was soon supplying retail shops all over the country. To meet the demand he gath-

ered about him a small team of photographers, and published the work of independent artist-photographers of the calibre of Roger Fenton and Francis Bedford. In order to gain some understanding of the scale of Frith's business one only has to look at the catalogue issued by Frith & Co in 1886: it runs to some 670 pages, listing not only many thousands of views of the British Isles but also many photographs of most European countries, and China, Japan, the USA and Canada - note the sample page shown here from the hand-written Frith & Co ledgers recording the pictures. By 1890 Frith had created the greatest specialist photographic publishing company in the world, with over 2,000 sales outlets - more than the combined number that Boots and WH Smith have today! The picture on the next page shows the Frith & Co display board at Ingleton in the Yorkshire Dales. Beautifully constructed with mahogany frame and gilt inserts, it could display up to a dozen local scenes.

POSTCARD BONANZA

The ever-popular holiday postcard we know today took many years to develop. In 1870 the Post Office issued the first plain cards, with a pre-printed stamp on one face. In 1894 they allowed other publishers' cards to be sent through the mail with an attached adhesive halfpenny stamp. Demand grew rapidly, and in 1895 a new size of postcard was permitted called the court card, but there was little room for illustration. In 1899, a year after Frith's death, a new card measuring 5.5 x 3.5 inches became the standard format, but it was not until 1902 that the divided back came into being, so that the address and message could be on one face and a full-size illustration on the other. Frith & Co were in the vanguard of postcard development: Frith's sons Eustace and Cyril continued their father's monumental task, expanding the number of views offered to the public and recording more

(handwritten ledger)
St Catherine's College
Senate House & Library
Gerrard Hostel Bridge
Geological Museum
Addenbrooke's Hospital
St Mary's Church
Fitzwilliam Museum, Pitt Press &c
Buxton, The Crescent
The Colonnade
Public Gardens
Haddon Hall, View from the Terrace
Miller's Dale

and more places in Britain, as the coasts and countryside were opened up to mass travel.

Francis Frith had died in 1898 at his villa in Cannes, his great project still growing. The archive he created continued in business for another seventy years. By 1970 it contained over a third of a million pictures showing 7,000 British towns and villages.

FRANCIS FRITH'S LEGACY

Frith's legacy to us today is of immense significance and value, for the magnificent archive of evocative photographs he created provides a unique record of change in the cities, towns and villages throughout Britain over a century and more. Frith and his fellow studio photographers revisited locations many times down the years to update their views, compiling for us an enthralling and colourful pageant of British life and character.

We are fortunate that Frith was dedicated to recording the minutiae of everyday life. For it is this sheer wealth of visual data, the painstaking chronicle of changes in dress, transport, street layouts, buildings, housing, engineering and landscape that captivates us so much today. His remarkable images offer us a powerful link with the past and with the lives of our ancestors.

THE VALUE OF THE ARCHIVE TODAY

Computers have now made it possible for Frith's many thousands of images to be accessed almost instantly. Frith's images are increasingly used as visual resources, by social historians, by researchers into genealogy and ancestry, by architects and town planners, and by teachers involved in local history projects.

In addition, the archive offers every one of us an opportunity to examine the places where we and our families have lived and worked down the years. Highly successful in Frith's own era, the archive is now, a century and more on, entering a new phase of popularity. Historians consider the Francis Frith Collection to be of prime national importance. It is the only archive of its kind remaining in private ownership. Francis Frith's archive is now housed in an historic timber barn in the beautiful village of Teffont in Wiltshire. Its founder would not recognize the archive office as it is today. In place of the many thousands of dusty boxes containing glass plate negatives and an all-pervading odour of photographic chemicals, there are now ranks of computer screens. He would be amazed to watch his images travelling round the world at unimaginable speeds through internet lines.

The archive's future is both bright and exciting. Francis Frith, with his unshakeable belief in making photographs available to the greatest number of people, would undoubtedly approve of what is being done today with his lifetime's work. His photographs depicting our shared past are now bringing pleasure and enlightenment to millions around the world a century and more after his death.

LANCASHIRE VILLAGES

AN INTRODUCTION

OLD STORIES and beliefs die hard. There are still many people who think of Lancashire and its villages as drab, harsh, bleak and persistently wet. Nothing could be further from the truth. Although fragments of beauty have been lost in local government boundary changes, Lancashire has gained other scenic gems; and those enthusiasts still clamouring for the old order to be reinstated may yet be rewarded.

In the reign of King Alfred, all Lancashire was divided into six areas, or Hundreds. The Fylde, or Hundred of Amounderness, formed one third of the whole, stretching between two rivers, the Ribble and the Wyre, from the coast to the hills of nether Wyresdale. The other Hundreds were Blackburn, Leyland, Lonsdale, Salford and West Derby.

Even before the Industrial Revolution, people from agricultural communities were forced to find work in commercial centres, which later burgeoned into some of the greatest cities in the land. Lancashire was very much based on village settlements, some of which had existed long before they were recorded in the Domesday

Book (1085-86). William the Conqueror was curious to know what he had conquered after the Battle of Hastings in 1066, and he sent commissioners into every hundred to record in detail what they found. Many areas had suffered from pestilence, war and famine; this is borne out in a bleak summing up of the area that became the Fylde (the name derives from 'gefilde', meaning 'field'). In three pages of Latin, the inventory states that the Hundred of Amounderness was 'sparsely populated and laid waste'. Easily recognizable village names stare from the parchment: 'Carlentum', 'Torentum', Biscopham', 'Poltun'. Domesday remains a vital source for understanding the origins of modern society. Certainly William was fortunate to inherit a good system of land tenure set up by the Anglo-Saxons.

Why was so much of coastal and inland Lancashire designated wasteland? One important reason lay in the vast tracts of marsh or 'moss', land which remained unproductive until efficient drainage was carried out by 19th-century landlords – by draining Thornton Marsh, Bold Fleetwood Hesketh had led the way in the 18th century. However, it is useful to remember that this inhospitable territory could serve as refuge for felons, hostile tribes, or those fleeing from religious persecution. It was dangerous country, but small settlements survived on a bountiful supply of fish, flesh and fowl.

The medieval abbot of Cockersand refused to carry out his visitation to the monks of the abbey without a competent guide across Pilling Moss, for although a learned man, he associated the flickering blue lights of marsh gas not with their scientific cause, but with necromancy. His first command was probably to order the monks to build Kate's Pad, a causeway of riven oaks. Lying six feet below the surface of the marsh, it was discovered in the 19th century along with ancient tools, urns, and huge moss stocks, the giant trees of a forest laid low by the rush of the sea inland. One oak alone took three days to move.

As the years rolled by, the robust quality of Lancashire people was exemplified by a troop of brilliant men and women: thinkers, free spirits,

inventors, entertainers, soldiers and sailors, moralists, reformers, statesmen, musicians, and men of letters and of science. The weft and warp of centuries formed the nature of Lancashire's inhabitants, who are now universally known for friendliness, generosity and a warm sense of humour. Good judges of character, the feisty villagers looked men in the eye and did not suffer fools gladly. In the race for firsts, Lancashire was leader: many a pioneer in the fields of health, education, the railways, the canals, the co-operative movement, free libraries and free trade came from the villages.

Picture a ten-year-old boy, Edward Baines, born in 1774, who set off from his village of Walton-le-Dale with pupils from Preston Grammar School. He was fired by a scheme to found a school in North America, and his goal was Liverpool, where ships sailed to the New World. Was his enterprise that of a questing spirit, or was it just daft, as we say in Lancashire? That boy in adult life published a gazetteer of Lancashire towns and villages, a detailed, economic and social picture produced at a time of great change. Baines's 'Lancashire' is probably more consulted than the Domesday Book.

Lancashire villages developed according to circumstances, and according to the richness or paucity of natural resources like wood or stone. Once the marshlands so feared by the abbot were tamed, becoming 'the cornfield of Lancashire' and 'the breadbasket of Manchester', early tourism reared its head. Canals and rivers gave further impetus to progress. A host of picturesque villages, self-sufficient and eager to supply fresh demands, grew from tiny hamlets. Great Singleton, Roseacre, Wharles, Treales, Esprick, Medlar, and Thistleton, for instance,

were beloved of artists for their thatched cottages, genuine Fylde 'peasants' and roses round the door. Mrs Swarbrick and Mrs Hardman, famed respectively for Wardleys toffee and best butter, were known beyond Lancashire, and 'Old Doilee' (Dolly) was famous too for her sought-after strawberry and cream teas. Loaded wagonettes came to Hambleton for succulent mussels hooked from the River Wyre, eventually to the point of extinction.

Allen Clarke, who pioneered cycling (the flat Lancashire plain was ideal for the new craze), put 'Windmill Land' on the map. Over forty peg, post or tower mills were busy grinding corn in one of the chief granaries of England. 'Rich meadows, good arable land, fine pastures cultivated with spirit and skill', declared one agrarian reformer. The poet Drayton exulted in this region of glorious sunsets, but the historian Camden deplored it as 'sore destitute of wood', unaware of those calamitous seas from the dark ages. Hard-headed farmers affirmed that 'clay upon sand makes land', and fertility did arise from the laying down of sand, gravel and thick layers of clay deposited from ancient seas.

Nowadays, swift traffic bowls along country lanes hedged with hawthorn white as snow in spring, their winding course formed by herds of cattle from the north grazing behind their drovers. This area was famous for Longhorns. Geese destined for Poulton-le-Fylde (which was known as the metropolis – its markets drew people from miles around) had their webbed feet coated with tar to withstand the journey, their indignant cries floating over the fields to mingle with larks' song, the cries of curlews and the clack of windmill sails. Winding lanes also led to the high cliffs of Bispham. The windmill there, and the windmill on Rossall shore (shown on Yates's map of 1789), did not last long in 90mph gales and waves which could reach fifty feet high.

Cottages were built like Viking long houses, hugging the ground, safe retreats for man and beast. Vernacular architecture used pebbles and boulders from the shore for walls and marram grass from the sand dunes for thatched roofs, while whole forked trees made supports (crucks) for gable ends. Clay and straw puddled and trampled by horses provided infilling; this ancient building material defies today's bulldozers, as does Roman mortar made from crushed shells.

Villagers trying to wrest a living from the cruel, capricious Irish Sea deemed wrecks their right, but by law they belonged to the lord of the manor. The constant battle against the incursion of the seas pounding a long coastline called for the greatest character and ingenuity of all. Villages were washed away, including Fenny, Singleton Thorpe, Singleton Wyke, Kilgrimol, Argameols and the manor of Chornet, which was owned by the Lords of Rossall. The villagers of Singleton Thorpe probably fled for their lives in 1588 when rough seas scattered the galleons of the Spanish Armada; the remains of cottages and a village inn were found in archeological digging two centuries ago. It is good to know that

the indomitable few who survived 'set up shop', to use a Lancashire expression, inland at Great and Little Singleton, which rose phoenix-like not from ashes but from salt water.

The sea-bathing craze of the 18th and 19th centuries found coastal villages only too ready to grasp a new trade in all its aspects. Nowhere is this better illustrated than in the phenomenal rise of Blackpool, once an unknown hamlet where a peat-brown stream trickled into the Irish Sea. Seven miles of golden sand were exploited. Supplies of food for the invading hordes came from Poulton, which had quickly thrown off its sleepy, muddy duck-pond image and was feverishly beckoning Charles Dickens, John Bright, Keir Hardie and other notables to view its well-preserved medieval trappings (a tithe barn, a market cross, stocks, fish stones and a whipping post).

But what of the stone villages, those up hill and down dale settlements? Back in the mists of time, the Segantii tribe ('dwellers in the waters') and the Brigantes had followed the ridgeways, for this was good look-out country; the Romans and the New Army of Oliver Cromwell followed their example. This high, dry land was clear of the marshland, and villages arose. Quarried stone went into the cottages and the strong-built

yeomen's farm houses standing foursquare to the winds of Pendle and Bowland. In the pastures of Wyresdale lay the famous vaccaries, where cattle flourished. When the farmers pulled down their barns to build greater ones, they could not resist taking stone from ruined abbeys and castles (Cockersand, Whalley, Clitheroe, and Greenhalgh, for instance). Imagine the consternation in a village where the baker in charge of the communal oven used an old gravestone on which to knead the dough - the impression of a death's head appeared on his batches of bread!

The industrial areas of Lancashire were sprinkled with villages which had managed quite well until machinery banished their way of life. Machine-made nails supplanted hand-made ones, which threw the villagers of Hardhorn and many other places into despair, until they adapted. Handloom weavers at Wycoller, Dolphinholme and Freckleton were reduced to beggary. Poverty wiped some villages out entirely. James Thompson, a calico printer of Primrose Mill near Clitheroe, stated in the House of Commons in 1833 that handloom-weaving families making coarse cotton cloth with two looms could earn no more than six shillings a week. They were hopelessly poor even before the advent of machinery. The desperation of the machine breakers (disciples of the Luddite movement) was understandable, but punishment was swift and harsh. At Mellor, the village blacksmith made pikes for villagers involved in machine breaking. Spinning and weaving had been a main cottage industry until power looms were invented at the beginning of the Industrial Revolution. Inevitably, villagers had to adapt, and many went to work in the mills.

Because of its profitable coach trade, Garstang fought against the coming of the railway. Its railway station was now a mile away, of little use to trade, but the village remained important for its cattle and horse trading - weekly markets were traditionally held on a Thursday. Scorton village was barred from any change by the lord of the manor. It had no inn, no school, and no police constable, but as the gateway to the forest of Bowland and the Trough leading to Dunsop Bridge, its popularity never waned, even when its silk and bobbin mill failed.

But there could be another side to the coin where villages gained a new raison d'etre. For instance, visitors in wagonettes and early charabancs rolled up to Preesall to view the much-talked-of rose gardens grown by Vicar Kendall, who usually presided over the parish wearing a black panama hat to tone with his clerical robes. The village's alarming reputation for subsidence was due to the salt mines, and villagers lived dangerously. Salt of the finest quality was shipped away as far as India. The fame of an inhabitant could affect the fortunes of a village – an instance is the discovery of the transit of Venus by Jeremiah Horrocks of Hoole, near Preston on 14 December 1639. Jeremiah, also thought to be a vicar, blazed a trail for astronomy in England, and set the eyes of the world on a hitherto unknown hamlet.

Short of catastrophes like that at Tarnbrook in the 18th century, most villages survived; but here, unwittingly, hatters and glovers were poisoned and even driven mad by mercury, one of the tools of their trade. This was tragic indeed in a tiny, God-fearing community of Quakers, who came to Over Wyresdale to escape persecution. Isolated pockets of this large county attracted minority races and religions: black people worked in the silk or cotton mills at Galgate, Scorton and Ellel; Jewish tailors settled in the county; and so did Huguenots, driven from Europe by religious persecution. They settled and prospered, bringing new skills. Hard-working and intelligent, some proved to be the bedrock of their new community.

Wandering around Lancashire villages today, I have been struck by their huge diversity, by how much has survived unscathed, and by how fiercely tradition is defended. A good example is Downham, nestling in the shadow of Pendle Hill, where my grandmother was born. Talking to inhabitants, I am impressed by their keen interest in history. The evergreen memories of people whose families have never left the village serve as inspiration to the newcomers. Many of the latter become equally absorbed in local history, and set up or join local history societies dedicated to preserve and collect all the information and relevant artifacts they can about their newly adopted surroundings. Life has been breathed into the wonderful photographs in this book by a plethora of old-timers who remember, remember, remember … Eyes have sparkled, fingers have stabbed the air, mouths have opened wide and creased with both sadness and laughter. Such keen interest has set light to a train of memories and the desire to discover more.

In ways we cannot fully understand, old photographs act as a powerful stimulus to our memories. Street furniture, vehicles, trade signs, advertisements, tram lines, vanished shops, and so on, all provide a link with our identities and have become an integral part of every adult, even though these familiar things have slipped away. It is good and right that we should care and strive to preserve old photographs, bearing in mind one of the many sage sayings of the Chinese philosopher Confucius, who was born in 551BC: 'To understand the present, we must study the past'.

Time spent with old photographs is time well spent. Among the faces you might recognize one of your relations, as I did: gazing at a photograph of Blackburn Market taken in about 1900, I saw great-uncle Jonathan Cranshaw Houghton, a market inspector, standing alongside a fruit and vegetable stall; he was born in 1872.

THE PENDLE WITCHES TRAIL

ON THURSDAY 20 AUGUST 1612, three generations of so-called witches were marched through the crowded streets of Lancaster to a gallows on the moor one mile away. The clergyman in attendance intoned 'God show them mercy', but in their wretched lives they had been shown none. Poverty was perhaps their only crime; the charge of witchcraft was exacerbated by their accusers' ignorance and malice. This execution was the culmination of a long-standing feud between two families that ended in the destruction of each other.

The women were brought down by a mistaken belief in their own powers of black magic and by false testimony; but also the rare opportunity to be noticed and to have attention paid to them was irresistible, unaware as they were of King James I's new draconian laws against witchcraft. The fascinated interest in their fate and in the unexplained mysteries shrouding the event is as strong today as it was 500 years ago.

BARROWFORD, *The White Bear Inn c1950* B302028

Barrowford is where the Pendle Witches Trail begins. The forty-five mile route takes the visitor through historic villages and on to Lancaster Castle via the Trough of Bowland. This famous coaching inn is situated in that part of Barrowford which stretches along Gisburn Road, where many interesting old properties stand; it was built originally as the great house of the Hargreaves family, and it is the largest 17th-century building in the village. The datestone reads 1607, but 1697 is a more accurate date: the original datestone was misread owing to weathering when rebuilding of the inn took place in 1912. When John Hargreaves died in 1713, an inventory of his house was made room by room, from the milk house to the great parlour. The building has been an inn since 1775; the name no doubt refers to the cruel practice of bear baiting, a common entertainment in these days.

BARLEY
The Pendle Inn c1960
B892006

Standing at the foot of Pendle Hill, which is 1835ft high and just short of being a mountain, the stone-built Pendle Inn is in the centre of Barley, the heart of Pendle Witch country. Near the inn is a field which is said to have been used by the witches. Legend has it that the ground is poisoned, so the field has never been cultivated.

BARLEY, *The Village and Pendle Hill c1960* B892008

The ancient name for the village is Barelegh (meaning 'wasteland'), but lush meadows now support flocks of sheep. George Fox's vision on Pendle Hill in 1640 led to the founding of the Society of Friends. Two feuding families, the women ringleaders known as Chattox and Demdike, lived on the slopes of Pendle and became notorious for holding witches' covens. They were tried, with others, at Lancaster Castle. Ten people were hanged in August 1612. Demdike died in prison.

◀ **CHATBURN**
The Church 1894
34351

The village is 400ft above sea level off the A59. Its parish church, Christ Church, was erected in 1837, shortly after Queen Victoria came to the throne. The spire was struck by lightning in 1854 and the steeple had to be pulled down, but all was restored and the church extended in 1882. Silver Roman coins have been found here, as the Roman route to Ribchester is close by.

◄ BLACKO
The View from Noggarth c1960
B442023

Blacko Tower (just visible on the top of the hill), marking the boundary of Pendle Forest, was built by Jonathan Stansfield in 1891. Jonathan 'wearied in well doing', and a troop of Boy Scouts from Colne eventually finished the structure. It is thought to be on the site of Malkin Tower, where Mother Demdike and her witch companions hid before capture. Other towers in the area are Grant's Tower, Peel Tower, Darwen Tower and Hampsfell, mainly popular tributes to Queen Victoria.

▲ **CHATBURN,** *Sawley Road c1950* C462001

The homes in the stone-built terrace (right) were once fitted with hand-looms, but the end cottage with the sign sold tyres at the time of the photograph. Some villagers from here worked in the corn mill converted to cotton spinning. A great spirit prevailed amongst the mill workers, who particularly enjoyed Christmas parties at the mills. My grandmother remembered Whitsuntide processions passing the Black Bull inn. Grandfather recalled the quack doctor of Chatburn who sold 'universal pills'; the doctor was drowned at the age of 80 as he tried to ford the river. On 30 October 1940 German bombs fell on the village post office and cottages. Miss Robinson, one of the people killed, left a field for the villagers in her will, which was used to commemorate Queen Elizabeth's coronation in 1953 as the village playing fields.

◄ CHATBURN
Gisburn Road c1950
C462005

The sign tells us that Gisburn Road leads to Clitheroe, hub of the Pendle Forest area. Stone walls, finials, setts, dripstones and lintels characterise Chatburn and the neighbouring villages. Laura described busy mill days: 'We wove miles of Chatburn checks … it was dobby weaving, which went into turbans out East and tea towels out at Colne!' The Brown Cow and the Black Bull, built in 1855, were voted 'excellent', as was Hudson's ice cream shop, which was housed in what was originally the toll bar premises.

▶ **CHATBURN**
*Downham Road
c1950* C462006

This part of Chatburn, leading to Downham, is reminiscent of the many stone villages hereabouts, which according to legend and tradition are steeped in witchcraft. Chatburn, like Worston Hall, was part of the Honour of Clitheroe. Nowadays, the notoriety of the witches of Pendle has created a lucrative tourist trade, and Witches Galore is a mecca for souvenir hunters. In 2003, the museum at Clitheroe Castle made a film about the witches' lives and deaths.

◀**CHATBURN**
General View c1950
C462007

Two miles from Clitheroe, Chatburn is well sheltered by a high ridge and a wealth of trees. Quarrying and textile industries are still carried on here, but for centuries the villagers were mainly workers on the land. Chatburn ran a Friendly Society, or Blanket Club, in about 1750. Housing estates now cover areas where once busy mills throbbed.

▲ **DOWNHAM,** *The Church 1921* 71183

Listed by Edward Baines in his Gazetteer with the many villages of Blackburn Hundred, Downham is 3 miles north-east of Clitheroe. The church of St Leonard has a tower of 15th-century origin, but there has been a church on this site since the 13th century. The main part of the church dates from 1910, when some buildings in Downham were rebuilt. A custom was still being observed in 1930 that had run for 250 years: the Assheton sermon was preached by the Rev J A Latham, vicar of Read. This sermon, referred to as the 'Downham preaching', was delivered annually on 30 January. The church faces the Assheton Arms, and since the 17th century the Assheton family has controlled the village from Downham Hall.

◄**DOWNHAM**
The Village and Pendle Hill 1921 71187

This ancient and beautiful village dates back to Saxon times. The beacon on Pendle Hill is said to be Saxon, and the field known as Kirkacre was in existence when Alfred the Saxon was chieftain. Today's grey stone or white-washed cottages were built in the 18th and 19th centuries for handloom weavers. Where the brook runs through the village, each cottage had a stone slab to cross. Sir Ralph Assheton purchased a fine example of a 'Downham diamond' for only five shillings in the 17th century. Found in the local limestone, these were large quartz crystals. A flagstone path has been laid on Pendle Hill to combat erosion. Every Hallowe'en the thrill of the witches of Pendle lures enthusiasts carrying lanterns to ascend. At Longridge this was called 'lating of the witches'.

DOWNHAM
The Village 1921
71188

A small group (centre left), seeking the shade of mature trees in the hot summer of 1921, faces the photographer. The steep slope of the village street leads to a second group of cottages clustered round the village green. To the right, up three steps, is the entry to St Leonard's churchyard. Three of the five bells hanging in the church tower date from the 15th century.

DOWNHAM, *Top Row c1955* D166008

The mullioned windows (right) may indicate that the building is of Tudor origin. The second cottage on the left in this typical row is, I believe, where my grandmother was born. She worked for the Garnett family of Low Moor. The Roman road, where the remains of two Roman soldiers were found, was near Top Row.

BOLTON-BY-BOWLAND
The Church 1921
71209

The church of St Peter and St Paul dates from the 13th century, but the magnificent tower was rebuilt in 1852. Inside is a memorial to a local knight, Sir Ralph Pudsay, who had twenty-five children. Bolton Hall, where once King Henry VI stayed in hiding, has now gone, but the gateposts can still be seen opposite the church.

BOLTON-BY-BOWLAND, *The Stocks and the War Memorial c1955* B856002

The village is listed in the Domesday Book as Bodeton. The great age of the market cross, with its uneven steps and remains of the punishment stocks, is apparent. A Market Charter was granted in the 14th century. The group stands in what is the smaller but definitely the older of the two village greens. In 1970 a village hall was built to accommodate the varied activities of a growing population.

▼ **BOLTON-BY-BOWLAND,** *Yew Tree Cottages c1955* B856005

The cottages and mature trees are typical of Bolton-by-Bowland. This beautiful village, once famous for its skilled bowmen, stands on the edge of Bowland Forest. The school, built of local limestone, replaced a school which had stood on the Green since 1620. This village green was also the site of the court house. Hatters, shoemakers and corn millers, along with stonemasons, joiners and blacksmiths, kept the village well supplied in the 19th century.

▶ **BOLTON-BY-BOWLAND**
The Village c1955
B856008

This part of the village is immediately behind the church. Bolton Hall Estate own most of the property here; no new houses have been built, nor is there employment other than in agriculture. In 1865, when the estate was owned by a Mr Wright, he employed almost the whole village as workers.

◄ **BOLTON-BY-BOWLAND**
The Village from the Church Tower c1955 B856016

This excellent view from the church tower shows the whole village and its rural surroundings. The tower, unusual architecturally for this part of Britain, is thought to have been influenced in style by King Henry VI during his stay in Bolton Hall. King Henry's Well (a circular stone building where he bathed) still stands, but the Hall was demolished in 1950. The solitary motor coach is a sign of visiting sightseers.

► **GISBURN**
The Church 1921
71201

The church of St Mary is glorious with snowdrops in winter. An unusual headstone is that of Jenny Preston, showing a witch with her cauldron. Gisburn appears in Domesday Book. The church tower looks Norman, but the main doorway is 13th-century. Oliver Cromwell stabled horses and troops in the church after the Battle of Preston in 1648.

DUNSOP BRIDGE
The Entrance to Brennand Valley 1921 71225

This village at the entrance to the Trough of Bowland has officially been declared the nearest village to the centre of the British Isles. A telephone box marks the spot. The Pendle witches travelled through the Trough to Lancaster for judgement. Brennand Valley is just one of many beauty spots threading the fells near Dunsop Bridge. In Slaidburn's Church Street there is a plaque stating that the school there was endowed and erected by John Brennand, a much-respected benefactor, who died in 1717.

DUNSOP BRIDGE, *St Hubert's Church 1921* 71227

The pure white marble angel (centre left) is seen by all who pass through the Trough of Bowland. Less well known is the painting on the ceiling above the altar showing Kettledrum, a famous racehorse and winner of the 1861 Derby. Owned by the Townley family, Kettledrum was reared at Stud Farm. A trout hatchery is now on the site of another old stables. Indeed, St Hubert's, the Townleys and horse racing are so traditionally linked that villagers feel that Kettledrum's winnings paid for building the church.

GRINDLETON
Stone Hill and the Post Office c1960 G64003

The fells sheltering this village, most of which lies at the foot of this steep main street, rise to 1,000ft. The rest of the village follows the high road above the River Ribble. In the 19th century and later, the village was busy with spinning and weaving, a felt hat works and a jam factory - the population was twice that of the 20th century. This scene is remarkably traffic-free except for one motor car (left). At the post office (center left), reached by a narrow ginnel, Wall's ice cream is sold.

GRINDLETON
The Village c1960 G64004

Two bus stops are opposite each other: one is outside the shop advertising Zebrite, a black lead used to clean iron grates and the ranges found in most cottages. The circular window in the stone building (right) is a witch window. Some houses had ledges fitted near chimneys for a witch to rest upon and be appeased. It was always wise to keep on the right side of a witch - their malice was a real fear in Pendle country!

◄NEWCHURCH IN PENDLE
The Village c1960
N191012

This Pennine hill village had a chapel in 1216. It became a flourishing handloom weaving village - in all there were about 400 looms, and some villagers coupled weaving with farming - but when machines supplanted their skills, there was much suffering. There are two inns: the Lamb Inn (left) on the crest of the hill, and the second next to the café (right).

◀ **LANGHO**
St Mary's Church
c1965 L290030

At the foot of Langho Fells and in sight of Pendle Hill stands the Saxon village of Old Langho; its church, St Leonard's, was built with stone that came from Whalley Abbey in about 1530. The newer part of Langho, about a mile distant, has developed since the road to Clitheroe from Blackburn was made. York Lane, part of the Roman road to Ribchester, has yielded up Roman coins, and tales linger of the ghosts of Roman soldiers. St Mary's church, a pleasant modern building, is amongst the new estates which have appeared since 1960. The late Jessica Lofthouse, the traveller and historian, lived at Langho.

▲ **NEWCHURCH IN PENDLE**
The Village c1960 N191011

This village is at the very heart of so called 'witch country'. Its 16th-century church has the Eye of God on its church tower to protect the villagers against witchcraft, which was so genuinely feared by the parishioners of St Mary's. A rush bearing procession is still observed annually; this dates from the days when the rush-cart brought fresh rushes to strew on the earth floors. We can see that the village lies on a slope; Pendle Hill rises behind.

◀ **NEWCHURCH IN PENDLE**
The Witch's Grave c1960
N191017

Alice Nutter is said to be buried here. On 27 April 1612, at Read Hall, Justice Nowell questioned James, Jennet and Elizabeth Device about a witches' Sabbath, and they stated that Alice Nutter of Roughlee Hall was a participant. Rumour said it was not so, for Alice was of a different calibre to the rest. Nevertheless she was sent to Lancaster Prison, and watched by thousands she was hanged on 20 August with the others accused on Lancaster Moor.

UP HILL AND DOWN DALE

THE HIGHEST village in Lancashire is Belthorn near Blackburn, where my father was born. On a clear day villagers could see Blackpool Tower and the Lancashire coast. On Shrove Tuesdays, when pancakes were tossed, a good pinch of snow went into the batter. Snow could be relied upon in March, 900 ft above sea level.

From the stage coaches which ran between the inns, the villages and the great houses, the passengers could see castles on distant hillsides. Sandstone milestones, triangular in shape with sloping tops engraved with distances and destinations, cheered the traveller.

In the days when many people could neither read nor write, inn signs were useful with their pictures – the White Bear or the Golden Cockerel, for example. The sign of a large wooden hand nailed on to a barn door meant there was a fair in progress in that village. Brandy snap stalls, pedlars with ribbons and laces, frumenty and gingerbread sellers, and wig makers on the lookout for ladies willing to sell their hair - all these made for a lively scene.

GRINDLETON, *The Village 1899* 43494

This is truly an 'up hill and down dale ' village, for half is at the bottom of a hill, the other half high above the River Ribble. The church of St Ambrose stands on the Sawley Road next to the school. Set up by the photographer, the group outside the Buck Inn display a range of 19th-century garb: long skirts, long white aprons, and bowler, boater and trilby hats. Was that their Sunday best? The scene certainly enshrines the quiet, Sabbath calm of long ago.

▶ **BASHALL EAVES**
The Village c1955
B742008

Bashall Eaves stands on the banks of the river Hodder in the parish of Mitton. Many variations in its name (Bakesalf, Beckhalgh) speak of a long history, and so do 15th-century Bashall Hall, home of the powerful Talbot family, and the old Red Pump coaching inn and the remains of a corn mill run by John Halstead in 1822. Willows growing by Bashall Brook were used for basket making. The small farmstead (left) could have been an alehouse, like the one at Mason Green. The village observed old customs: Shrove Tuesday pancake collecting, and Collop Monday, when slices of bacon were begged for after pig killing. Belthorn was one of the last villages in Lancashire to honour Collop Monday, and Poulton-le-Fylde was the last to answer the call of the Pancake Bell.

◀ **BASHALL EAVES**
The Village c1955 B742009

Here we have another view of the village, with its cottages and barns built in its local sandstone. Stone lintels, dripstones above the windows fitted with 16 panes and glazing bars (left) go back to the days when Bashall Eaves was mainly self-supporting. Dry stone walls were built to last 100 years. Sett-paved yards (right) withstood iron-shod cart wheels. Villagers grew barley, fruit and vegetables, whilst the village shop supplied everything from treacle to paraffin oil. A string of itinerant tradesmen called: butcher, tinker, tailor, fishmonger, and muffin man. The blacksmith's shop and the wheelwright's were next to each other, and the smith obliged with extras: 'blowers' to 'wuther up' the fire and iron hoops for the boys to bowl.

▲ **CHIPPING,** *The Mill Pond c1955* C598015

In Lancashire, man-made stretches of water to serve mills were often called lodges. From the lodge, a channel or 'goit' carried water to the wheel. Berry's Chair Works and at one time Wolfen Mill used this mill pond. Chipping Brook once powered five water mills - one is now a restaurant called the Water Mill. Wolfen Mill made bobbins, then became a cheese factory. By about 1950 it was dilapidated, but it has since been made into a fine house.

◄**CHIPPING**
Wolfen House c1955
C598018

This was once the home of John de Knoll. The photograph shows Wolfen House after its transformation, in a beautiful woodland setting. Waterfowl, weasels, reed bunting, swallows and bats - and that lovely Bowland flower, the water flag - can be found here. Naturalists, cyclists and ramblers gather in the Cobbled Corner Café opposite the Sun Inn on Windy Street.

▼ **CHIPPING,** *The Church c1955* C598021

St Bartholomew's church dates back to 1240, but even before that there was a church on this high ground. The strong tower appeared in 1450. Within is a piscina, part of the original 12th-century building, and the font was probably presented by the Bradley family. Amidst such ancient relics the modern stained glass window celebrating the present-day Berry's Chairworks looks happily at home.

► **CHIPPING**
Windy Street and the Old School c1955
C598024

The building on the right jutting into Windy Street is John Brabin's school. He was a great benefactor; his home was on Chipping's main street at what is now the post office. Brabin, who died in 1683, was a dealer in cloth, and he made a fortune dyeing cloth with splendid hues. The old school is now a youth club. John Brabin left money to build a school and pay for books and schoolmaster.

◀ DOLPHINHOLME
Corless Cottages c1950
D210004

The name Corless is associated with the family who lived at Springfield House, Pilling. James Derham owned Corless Mill in Nether Wyresdale, 6 miles from Lancaster, and in 1801 he manufactured gas to light the mill and his workers' cottages. Dolphinholme was the first village to be lit by gas, and its first gas lamp is preserved at Derham House. At its peak the mill employed 1400 people, who worked shifts, day and night. Four hundred of these workers combed wool in their homes at Forton, Scorton and Nether Wyresdale. The lavish use of stone in these cottages (it came from quarries at Tootle Heights near Longridge) was made possible by the plentiful supply in those days. This 19th century terrace is typical of Lancashire villages in this region backed by long ridges of Pennine hills. It is identical to Club Row in Longridge, which only came about through the tenacity of twenty Lancashire quarry workers who saved up and built the terrace.

➤ DOLPHINHOLME
Pennine View c1950
D210006

The houses on Pennine View are from a different era to the ones we saw in D210004, and catering for more modern workers. This upper part of the village is situated in the foothills of the Pennine Chain. Lower Dolphinholme is closer to the river and the worsted spinning mill, whose vast wheel was driven by water from the River Wyre. The mill closed in 1867.

◄ **DOLPHINHOLME**
The Cinder Path
c1950 D210008

This track could be part of the route along which came supplies of wool for Dolphinholme Mill. Horse-drawn carts and heavy wagons ascending the hill to the factory needed some of the workforce to push the heavy loads. Mr W Winder, the church clerk, has a chest of drawers made from a hand loom which once supplied the mill. Instruments for combing and carding wool have been found at farms nearby.

◄ **DOLPHINHOLME**
*St Mark's Church
c1950* D210007

The parish church of St Mark is in the main part of the village, near the Methodist Chapel, the primary school and the village shop. Before the factory came, there was nothing here but farmland, moorland and Fenton Cawthorne's tower. Now, the factory warehouse has been converted into flats, the great Wyresdale wheel dismantled and Wyresdale Tower pulled down, and its stones carted away. Fenton's proud boast carved in the stone that 'This Tower shall live in song and Wyresdale is its name' is now used as a doorstep in Abbeystead.

▲ **HURST GREEN,** *From Sandrock c1955* H445009

Between Preston and Clitheroe lies Hurst Green in the Ribble Valley, backed by Longridge fells. It was always a popular tourist village, and there were two ferries over the Ribble, Trough House and Hacking Boat. The Shireburns were great benefactors here; Richard Shireburn provided almshouses and a school, and the family lived at what became Stonyhurst College. Farming was long a way of life, but handloom weaving occupied many villagers, with local bobbin mills supplying the industry.

◄ **HURST GREEN**
The Cross c1950
H445011

Teas with Hovis bread, Ellis Wilkinson's mineral waters, Pyper's Ices, sweets, fruit drinks, teas and refreshments were all obtainable by the cross at Hurst Green. The striped cabin (right) supplied cigarettes, and down the main street was the Eagle and Child inn. Again we see an empty road, but motor traffic has made an appearance in the form of two parked motor cars, one alongside a striped sign post to Clitheroe.

▼ **HURST GREEN,** *The Barley Arms and the Village c1955* H445030

The Barley Arms (right) is an 18th-century inn with stone quoins and stone window surrounds. It is one of three attractive inns, which must add to the popularity of the village. The weather is not so harsh here, as the area is protected by Longridge Fell. The Shireburn family were also protectors. Sir Nicholas brought skilled weavers to his house at Stonyhurst to teach villagers textile weaving when times were hard, and he then supplied cottages with hand looms. The eldest son of the Shireburn family was always christened Edward.

► **PENDLETON**
The Church 1921 71163

The church of All Saints at the east end of the village began as a chapel in 1847, increasing in size fifty years later. Opposite was one of the first National Schools to open, but it is no longer in use as a school. Trees abound in the churchyard, along with gravestones bearing familiar local names. But one pauper, Jeppe Knave, who was found murdered, could not find room in the graveyard: no person or authority would pay for his burial.

◄ PENDLETON
The Village c1955
P25006

An ancient village recorded in the Domesday Book as Penictune, it has a stream flowing through it like Downham has, and it also lies at the foot of Pendle Hill. Fiddle Bridge, a large stone, formed a way across the water – it is now overgrown. Devil's Bridge was used for packhorses. Post Office Row (right) is remembered for Ellen Haworth, a diminutive lady. She was the schoolmaster's daughter, who kept the post office in 1890, and never left the village. At the end of this 18th-century row was a well, the village water supply. The pure spring water of Pendle is still favoured for home-brewed ales.

► RIMINGTON
Newby c1955 R273001

The hamlets of Stopper Lane, Martin Top, Newby and Howgill comprise this small, scattered community recorded in Domesday Book. Francis Duckworth in the 19th century wrote a hymn that became so famous it was named after his village, and commemorated in a plaque. Rimington, along with Stopper Lane, was known for lead mining. Fluctuating Lancashire and Yorkshire boundaries have confused and annoyed villagers.

► **RIVINGTON**
The Barn c1955
R309006

This splendid barn was built as storage for hay. When Lord Leverhulme, the Sunlight Soap king, bought Hall Barn and Great House Barn he had them renovated as public refreshment rooms. The only original components left of this ancient barn are its oak cruck supports. The area near Chorley has Bronze Age burial sites on the moors, indicating that it has been a settlement from ancient times. Like the one on Pendle Hill, the beacon on top of Rivington Pike is thought to have been lit when the Spanish Armada approached in 1588.

◄ **SLAIDBURN**
From the Bank 1921
71210

7 miles from Clitheroe on the banks of the River Hodder amidst moorland, Slaidburn is a popular village with walkers and cyclists. The view from the bank shows the 15th-century church of St Andrew. Its strong tower is 12th-century, and was used to shelter villagers when the Scots raided Lancashire. Brennand's Endowed School, built in 1717, stands next to the church.

▲ **SLAIDBURN,** *The Hark to Bounty Inn c1955* S139010

Between periods of calm, Slaidburn once resounded with noise; above the bustle rose the ringing bark of the squire's favourite hound Bounty. The name of the inn had to change! To this day the hunt meets outside. Up the flight of stone steps is the court room, in use until 1937. When the old court room crumbled, the officers of the village moved here, but the old benches were still there to tell of the room's old use.

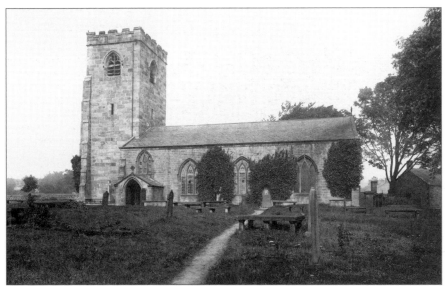

◄**WADDINGTON**
The Church 1899
42915

Stone from Waddington Fell was used to rebuild the church of St Helen in 1901. Only the tower of the old church remains - it dates back to c1500. That too was built from Waddington Fell stone. The Parker family of Browsholme, who have been connected with the village since the 16th century, are buried at Waddington.

WADDINGTON
The Almshouses 1921
71166a

Parker Almshouses, founded by Robert Parker in 1706, were later replaced by the ones we see here, which are built around a square. The homes of twenty-nine widows and spinsters, these pleasant houses are provided with a chapel. Robert Parker, a Yorkshire man, is not forgotten; his name is inscribed above the entrance as the original benefactor of Waddington Hospital. His birthday is also in the village calendar of events.

WADDINGTON, *The War Memorial 1921* 71167a

The war memorial is centrally placed in the village alongside the winding street by the stream. The roots of tradition run deep here, and some old customs were observed until the 19th century. Beating the parish bounds was important – the ceremony impressed upon young people the extent of the boundaries. The village still has its punishment stocks. Although the smithy is now a private house, older villagers recall the First World War and how the blacksmith was recruited on one day a week to make horse shoes for the war effort.

WADDINGTON
Coronation Bridge and the Church c1960 W523005

Coronation Gardens commemorate the crowning of Queen Elizabeth II. The flower beds are a riot of colour in high summer; they lie alongside the stream that runs through the main street. Trees and St Helen's church make a splendid backdrop. This view shows how the church looked after its rebuilding in 1901. Changes to the strong tower are the addition of a clock and finials to the four battlemented corners. In the tower hang 6 bells, cast in about 1760.

WARTON, *The View from the Crag 1918* 68313

Warton Crag is in an Area of Outstanding Natural Beauty; in a limestone region, it has an abundance of rare wild flowers, birds and mammals. The view of fields, fells, woods and rocky outcrops draws visitors, retired people, and naturalists looking for limestone pavements, such as the one in Eaves Wood. St Oswald's church, the rectory ruins and the Shovel Inn stand on the main street.

WARTON
Washington House
c1955 W30006

This is a favourite place of pilgrimage for loyal Americans. Washington House, on the main street, was the home of the forebears of American President George Washington. The stars and stripes flag is flown from the church tower every 4 July. Warton is a beautiful and thriving village, with a history going back to prehistoric times.

CATON, *The Village c1960* C473049

In the 1960s, the pace of building new housing quickened. Caton is popular as a retreat for commuters, who enjoy the moorland country near by with its fine views of Morecambe Bay. At the time of the Industrial Revolution there were cotton and bobbin mills here providing work for hundreds of operatives. Low Mill has been converted into flats. Willow Mill now provides offices and a craft centre.

CATON, *Croftlands c1955* C473026

Thomas Berry, a yeoman farmer, built this house on the site of an abbey in 1745. In 1833 one of his descendants refaced the stonework, commemorating this with a Latin inscription over the front door. For years Croftlands lay empty; then in 1928 it was bought by Colonel Walter Musgrave Hoyle, whose wife was the youngest daughter of Colonel Foster of Hornby Castle. Alterations were carefully made; Mrs Hoyle concentrated on the garden. Her restoration transformed the grounds into one of Lancashire's best gardens, and she also became Mayor of the City of Lancaster in 1938. In August 1961 she died, quite suddenly. Croftlands was sold by auction on 7 July 1976. In spite of its imposing facade, high walls and massive gates, Croftlands could well be missed by visitors hurrying to the Crook O' Lune beauty spot. Near here in1803 the discovery was made of a 6ft high Roman milestone, once important to the legions marching towards the fort in Lancaster.

CATON, *Hornby Road c1955* C473014

Stone-built cottages lend charm to Caton, which is proud of its ancient oak and fish stones. In the 1950s, Hornby Road featured Henty's confectioners and the post and telegraph office (left). The useful railway link with Wennington was lost in 1966, but the return of Caton's annual Gala, like the one at Poulton-le Fylde, was won by vociferous demand from villagers in about 1970. Caton once had an important market.

◄ **BROOKHOUSE**
General View c1960
B872046

Rows of stone cottages and rolling farmland characterise Brookhouse, which is close to Caton with Littledale and a popular retreat for commuters to Lancaster. New houses appeared between 1950 and 1960. Brookhouse has a plague stone at Bull Beck Bridge near the Black Bull Inn, and is proud of its proximity to Crook O' Lune, the famous beauty spot painted by Joseph Mallord Turner RA.

◀ **AUGHTON**
Church Lane
c1960 A350028

Mature trees line the lane leading to ancient St Michael's church, which has a Norman doorway. A fine view of the Welsh mountains can be had from the 14th-century spire set on a tower. Richard Massock's tomb is here – he was a Royalist captured at the Battle of Aughton Common. Aughton's sister church at Aughton Moss, Christ Church (known as the Cathedral on the Hill), has a rare Noah's Ark font.

▲ **SAWLEY ABBEY,** *The Abbey 1894* 34352

Only a ruin remains. Cistercian monks came from prosperous Fountains Abbey in 1148 to found Sawley, which is three miles from Clitheroe and by the river Ribble. They discovered that it was difficult to grow crops on the often waterlogged ground. The Dissolution of the Monasteries by Henry VIII led to the execution of the last abbot and the dispersal of the brothers. Stone from neglected Sawley Abbey was purloined and built into house walls – an example is the bay windows at 16th-century Little Mearley Hall near Pendleton. By 1904 the ruins were covered in ivy.

◀ **SAWLEY ABBEY**
The Cottages 1921
71146

The cottages in this idyllic scene by the River Ribble were at one time connected with a calico mill; they were later purchased and renovated by the Spread Eagle Hotel. Now let out as 'honeymoon cottages' (fully booked for Valentine's Day 2003), they have a new lease of life. The mature trees in the background were felled to provide room for 14 very expensive dwellings, but dredging of the river became necessary due to flooding.

SAWLEY ABBEY
The 'Roman' Arches
1921 71149

These arches can be seen when approaching Sawley (or 'Sally') Abbey. Built in about 1890, one of them had to be removed years later because it obstructed the highway. They were placed at the entrance to a field, and were rather more impressive than a gate! They appear to be partly old stone, along with a mixture of stone and statuary from other eras. In the 1980s, the Historical Society made a good job of tidying up the approach to Sawley Abbey, and one enthusiast is in attendance on Sundays (not in winter) to explain the ruins.

▼ **PLEASINGTON,** *The Priory Church 1894* 34324

Pleasington Priory, a Roman Catholic church dedicated to St Mary and John the Baptist and built in 1819, is set on a hill on Pleasington Lane, close to the River Dunsop and Witton Park, Blackburn. The priory is built in Gothic style. The large rose window and the doorway at the west end are impressive, as indeed is the whole building, with its handsome clerestory of 30 windows, its buttresses and statues, and its spacious interior.

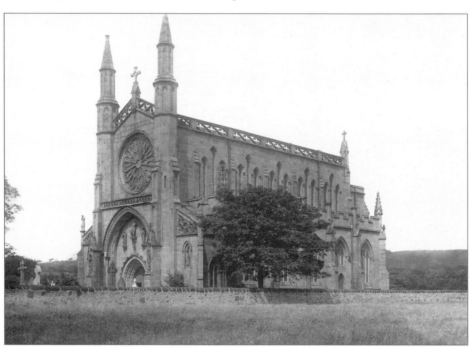

▶ **WRAY**

The River c1955 W588004

This busy mill, powered by the waters of the river Roeburn, ruled the lives of cottagers in the 17th and 18th centuries. Situated on the main street, many dated stone cottages housed the mill workers. The mill is now a private house. Captain Cuthbert Bradkirk came from Wray, near Carnforth. He was in charge of Clitheroe Castle after it was damaged by Prince Rupert's army. He repaired it, but he and his men had to leave hurriedly when news came that Cromwell's army was marching through the Ribble Valley.

◄ **WRAY**
General View
c1955 W588011

Still pleasantly rural, with views of woods and the distant Bowland Fells, this village stands near Wennington Hall, where Peter Hesketh, founder of Fleetwood-on-Wyre was born. The village still holds an annual fair and a Scarecrow Festival. On the main street stands Holy Trinity Church, built in 1840. The village experienced serious flooding in 1967 – flooding is always a threat, and cottagers use flood boards at their front doors. Quarrying, hand nail making, clog making and top-hat making have all gone, but one craft remains: swill (basket) making.

► **RIBCHESTER**
Stydd Church 1894
34328

It is said that this 'venerable' church, St Saviour's, is 900 years old, and that the apostle Paul preached here. It is also said that the origin of the name Stydd is 'stood', because during a severe earth tremor this was the only building undamaged. In 1866 a large outdoor service was held at this church; it can be reached through pleasant fields beyond the village of Ribchester.

RIBCHESTER
The New Hotel c1955
R29013

The Romans called their station here Bremetennacum Veteranorum in AD 80, and it was an important garrison. Today, so much interest is displayed in the Ribchester Roman Museum, which is devoted entirely to Roman history, that hotels remain busy, including the New Hotel. The tombstone of a cavalry rider and a replica of a parade helmet are what visitors come from far away to see. The original helmet, found by the river Ribble in 1796, is in the British Museum.

RIBCHESTER
The Recreation Ground
c1955 R29016

General Agricola established the Roman fort here, which grew into a thriving community. In the 18th century handloom and flax weaving became important. Modern Ribchester has also developed sports facilities, such as this recreation ground, which is useful on the Annual Field Day. Social groups include the Mothers' Union, the Over 60s Club, and the Amateur Theatrical Society. Behind the line of trees stands St Wilfred's church. 'The gift of a church' was made in about 1100 through Robert de Lacy, who held the Honour of Clitheroe.

RUFFORD, *Church Road c1955* R407011

This lovely, leafy village is situated near Southport. On the edge of the village stands the black and white half-timbered Rufford Old Hall, owned now by the National Trust, but seat of the Hesketh family for about 600 years. As lords of the manor, the Heskeths influenced village building, and were instrumental in draining the mosslands. In Church Road stands the 1869 Gothic-style church of St Mary, with monuments of past Heskeths brought from earlier churches.

SABDEN
Clitheroe Road c1960
S691018

On the left, Shell and Exide petrol pumps, a sign for Park Drive cigarettes, and new-style windows fitted into dwellings indicate progress. Wesley Street (right) is a reminder of the great Methodist preacher who encouraged the many chapels in the Ribble and Calder valleys. Most of these villages had Whitsuntide Walking Days, and Sabden was no exception. Hymn singing, the village band, a fair with swings and roundabouts, games and races, and washing baskets brimming with sandwiches were much enjoyed.

SABDEN, *The Caravan Site c1965* S691025

We can see Pendle Hill and Black Hill in the background. Beside Sabden Brook stands the church of St Nicholas, built in 1846. A countryside of varied beauty accounts for the caravan site. Popular Sabden attractions are Pendle Antiques Centre in Union Street and Pendle Toy and Train Museum. A favourite walk is down the valley between the rivers Calder and Ribble. The climb to the pass of Nick o' Pendle is another favourite.

SABDEN
Whalley Road c1955
S691009

A steep road from Sabden leads to the well-known pass of Nick o' Pendle. This essentially industrial village dating from the 17th and 18th centuries was on a pack horse route, but long before that Bronze Age traders came through. Richard Cobden's calico mill employed villagers from miles around in the 1830s. On the left, a striped post bearing the red torch of Lancashire County Council denotes a school ahead. Dressed stone walls, bay windows on the cottages, a corner shop, two early television aerials and motor traffic indicate that times are changing.

BRIDGES, CHURCHES AND OTHER TOUCHSTONES

A COUNTY of many rivers demands bridges, and most were built of quarried stone. Guided by two men, loaded sledges or 'sleds' were dragged down hillsides from the small quarries on Pendle Hill and Longridge and Waddington fells. The worn grooves made by this constant traffic are still visible today.

In past centuries, villagers shunned the responsibility of repairing bridges because of the expense on the parish. Rivers in spate roaring down could cause damage, and wooden bridges were the most vulnerable. (Beggars and illegitimate children were not welcome, again because caring for them was a cost to the parish. Paying tolls for the new turnpike roads was so resented that it could lead to bloodshed).

Touchstones came in many forms. Church gargoyles were carved with hideous expressions to frighten witches and evil spirits. Hagstones carved with the eye of God were built into barns and dairies for the same reason. Look out for millstones, punishment stocks, boundary crosses, pinfolds (cattle pounds), and remnants of Roman roads. Stone steps for mounting horses, 'upping stocks', are found outside churches, inns, and farmhouses. Some lock-ups were sited on bridges.

DUNSOP BRIDGE, *The Bridge c1960* D160005

This fine stone bridge is not unlike the one at Higher Brock. The Ribble Valley has many good examples, notably at Edisford and Halton, and Cromwell's bridge over the river Hodder. Because these old bridges were in constant use by pedestrians, coaches, pack horse trains, and carriers' carts, upkeep was important. The poles suspended beneath this bridge may be to catch debris when floods occur. Sometimes salmon nets or baulks were fixed, but only by licence.

DUNSOP BRIDGE
The Post Office
c1960 D160007

Here we have another view of the bridge. On the right is the post office; near here is the point that the Ordnance Survey declared was the centre of the British Isles. To mark the spot, they erected a public telephone box.

BASHALL EAVES, *The Post Office Café and General Stores c1955* B742010

The café is in the building at the top of the lane, with a post office and grocer's under the signs. Two miles from Clitheroe and near the River Hodder, the village has been subject to little change over the years. The Roman bridge can be found down a footpath near the post office, and Fairy Bridge is north of the Red Pump Inn.

▼ **OLD LANGHO,** *The Black Bull c1955* O139019

On the right, facing the village green, stands this old-world inn; the wide arch is the entry to a mews area for horse-drawn carts and carriages. Erected in 1554, this black and white timbered building is older than the church of St Leonard, which has carved stones that came from Whalley Abbey. This old church is now protected under the Redundant Churches scheme, and the Black Bull keeps the key.

► **GISBURN**

The Ribblesdale Arms c1950 G286002

The busy A59 road now divides Gisburn, but it still has its cobbled forecourts and white cottages in the main street. Here we will find the Ribblesdale Arms. The plaque above the doorway states that Thomas Lister bought the building in 1635 for 855 pounds. This inn is thronged with cyclists, walkers and visitors in the busy spring and summer months. This village's name was spelled 'Gisburne' until the railway arrived in 1885. The parish boundaries include Rimington, Newsholme, Nappa, Paythorne and other locations. An unusual grave can be found in the churchyard of St Mary - the opening notes of Francis Duckworth's famous hymn 'Rimington' are engraved on the stone. The 1710 tithe barn became a restaurant with a display of old farm utensils, similar to 'th'owd tithe barn' at Garstang. This is a region of salmon-rich rivers indeed, one apprentice complained that he was getting weary of eating salmon! On the Paythorne Road is the bridge where on Salmon Sunday villagers assemble to watch the fish swim and leap upstream.

◄ GISBURN
The Bridge 1921
71198

This strong two-arched stone bridge spans the River Ribble at Gisburn. Note the two farm carts with shafts designed for sturdy horses to the right of the yeoman farmer's dwelling. In this typically well-wooded river scene, we can see lavish use of stone in walls and bridge that could stand for centuries. A travelling mole catcher, Dick Cooper, lived in Gisburn; he covered the Ribble Valley and the Fylde, and walked the turnpike road between Blacko and Gisburn.

► SLAIDBURN
The Old Bridge 1921
71213

Overlooking the river is a village green which dwindles into a pleasant riverside walk along the Hodder. Uphill from the bridge are stone cottages. The Black Bull Inn became the Youth Hostel, and the Dog Inn is now the Hark to Bounty. Pack horse trains from different directions met at this point, the heart of Slaidburn in past centuries. Slaidburn has two magnificent bridges, this one over the unpolluted River Hodder, and the other crossing Croasdale Beck.

NEWTON
The Village 1921 71218

Because of its obscurity, this hamlet by the river Hodder was chosen by the Quakers as the site for their Friends' Meeting House, which was also used as a school in 1767 (right, with the tall belfry). Roads pass by leading to Dunsop Bridge and Slaidburn. The young John Bright attended school here to improve his knowledge and physique. He enjoyed country ways, and in manhood worked with another MP, Richard Cobden, to push the Reform Bills through Parliament. Both men championed the working classes.

► **GREAT MITTON**
The Churchyard, The Old Cross
1899 43495

The inscription on the base of this ancient cross tells us that it was renovated and re-erected 'To the glory of God and to commemorate the XIII hundredth year of the re-introduction of Christianity into Britain'. With a 15th-century tower, the church of All Hallows has sweeping views over surrounding country. It is thought that the chancel screen came from Sawley Abbey.

▼ **NEWTON-IN-BOWLAND**
The Village c1955 N190002

Three cars outside the Farmers Arms Inn indicate an increase in visitors to this 18th-century stone village. The women baked bread, washed clothes, used carved spoons made of sycamore wood (it did not stain), cared for children and eagerly awaited the weekly carrier's cart to replenish their stocks of candles, lamp oil and black lead. To be photographed would be a charming diversion!

► **GREAT MITTON**
The Post Office and the Church
1921 71152

The post office sign is visible over the lower window of the building immediately in front of the church. Amongst ancient artifacts at All Hallows church are a leper squint, a Jacobean pulpit, chained books and the tomb of Sir Richard Shireburne of Stoneyhurst. Yet another ancient cross base is located at Mitton Green. So often, these were from the original market cross.

◄ **HALTON**
From Castle Hill
c1955 H506007

An ancient settlement, Castle Hill near the church of St Wilfrid is the site of both Saxon and Roman fortifications. A Roman altar was discovered near the church in 1794, and in the 18th century a necklace and a hoard of coins were found, now in the British Museum. We can see 17th- and 18th-century houses in this scene. On clear days it is possible to see the rugged Forest of Bowland skyline - Wardstone, Clougha Pike and the neighbouring summits.

► **HALTON**
High Street c1955
H506012

P R Wright's draper's shop is to the far right, with a window display of clothes. Next to it is a high stone wall with an overgrown orchard or garden behind it, and then an old-fashioned telegraph pole with white porcelain pots on the crossbars. Opposite is the tobacconist's, also with a jam-packed display of pipes and cigars, and metal signs advertising Senior Service and Dunhill. It is noteworthy that half a century ago the High Street was empty of traffic. Baines's Gazetteer lists Matthew Redhead as landlord at the White Lion Inn in 1824.

◄ **HALTON**
Castle Road c1955
H506016

Halton on the River Lune (which finds its way out to sea at Lancaster) has developed into a commuter village. Halton Hall Park, beyond Castle Road, a 17th-century building, was altered c1850 when Robert F Bradshaw was lord of the manor. Kitchen ranges for houses large and small were supplied by Halton Foundry.

▲ **HORNBY,** *The Church 1896* 38268

St Margaret's church and the village lie in the Lune Valley, 9 miles from Lancaster. The church has a tower built by Sir Edward Stanley, Lord Monteagle to fulfil the vow he swore before his victory at Flodden Field in 1513 - his patron saint was St Margaret. (The song 'Flowers of the Forest' is a lament mourning the many Scottish dead who fell at that battle). Amongst the yew trees in the churchyard are medieval gravestones, one the well-known 'Loaves and Fishes' gravestone near the massive base of a Saxon cross. John Lingard, a Catholic priest who wrote a history of England, brought fame to Hornby - he died here in 1851.

◄ **HORNBY**
The Village c1955 H454008

Beneath massive trees a woman cyclist chats to a villager and her child (center left). On the right is the Castle Hotel, named after Hornby Castle overlooking the River Wenning. The lower parts of the tower date from the 13th century, but it was re-built in the 19th century. When the castle was left empty it became rat-infested. On my visit to the strong room, I was fascinated to see tiny pipistrelle bats. The railway station, demolished in 1968, stood on the old drove road leading to the fells we can just see in the background.

HORNBY
The Village c1955
H454013

Two motor cars are visible, but few street markings and signs, apart from the one on the right by the bow-windowed shop in the stone-built terrace. The road leads to the bridge over the River Wenning, which flooded two years ago. Beyond the bridge are the castle and the estate, and two churches, one the Roman Catholic church where John Lingard preached. There are many new houses here now, which are occupied by commuters to Lancaster and Heysham.

HORNBY
St Margaret's Church c1960 H454027

The tower of St Margaret's church is unusually-shaped in that it is octagonal. It was built by Lord Monteagle, who was also connected with the Isle of Man, so the arms of that island can be seen on the chancel. A new nave and a reredos with 20 angels are both noteworthy. Across the road is the war memorial built on the site of the old market cross; the market in medieval times was protected by the castle.

CROSTON, *The War Memorial c1950* C474003

The squire here, Sigismund de Trafford of Croston Hall, said that he 'preferred trees to chimneys', and was opposed to selling land for industrial development. The de Trafford family dated back to the Norman Conquest. Their preference for country traditions, such as maypole dancing, fairs, festivals and Armistice Day gatherings round Croston war memorial, account for the peacefulness of the village and for many trees, in particular an avenue of ancient limes.

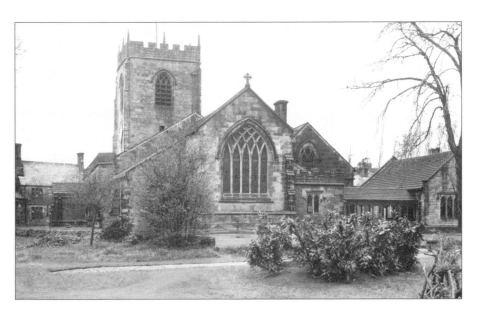

CROSTON
*The Parish Church
c1950* C474005

Croston lies on the banks of the River Yarrow, 10 miles from Preston. Cobbled Church Street leads to the church of St Michael and All Angels - the parish boundaries once extended to Chorley. At the end of this street is the ancient base of a restored preaching cross. The blacksmith's forge used to be there too. 18th- and 19th-century sandstone houses, a village green and a pack horse bridge add to Croston's charm.

CROSTON, *The Rectory Ruins c1950* C474006

The name 'Croston' means 'town with a cross'. The Croston Hall squires much influenced the running of the village, but they became impoverished; the Hall eventually fell into rack and ruin under the last squire, Captain Geoffrey de Trafford. Although the Hall was demolished, a chapel designed by the famous architect August Welby Pugin survived. The rectory also fell into ruin – the ruins act as an unusual gateway to the new rectory in the background. One rector presided for 66 years. The Bishop of Whalley lived here in 1920.

► **HOGHTON**
*The Tower
Courtyard 1895*
35720

Hoghton Tower, set on a hill and visible for miles, dates from 1565. King James I beggared the Hoghtons by overstaying on a visit with all his retainers. On 17 August 1617, having enjoyed his meal in the banqueting hall the king knighted a loin of beef, playfully announcing 'Rise, Sir Loin'. Tradition says that the long drive from the road to the top of the hill was covered with a welcoming carpet. In the 18th century, the village of Hoghton was a centre of handloom weaving, and the almost derelict Hoghton Tower was let as tenements; but it is now well restored and popular with tourists, many from abroad.

◄ **HOGHTON**
Bottoms Viaduct 1895
35722

This splendid photograph of this beauty spot was taken from a point on what is now called Witton Weavers Way, the Beamers Trail in picturesque Witton Park close to Blackburn. In the shadow of Woodcock Hill with the River Darwen flowing beneath, the viaduct also spans the valley floor with its wealth of mature trees. Pleasington Priory and Billinge Hall are within reach further along the 6-mile trail.

▲ **BALDERSTONE**, *Commons Lane c1955* B852004

Balderstone Grange and Balderstone CE Primary School stand on Commons Lane, which eventually joins Higher Commons Lane. In this still mainly rural area, names redolent of the country abound: Pewter House Fold, Smalley Fold, Hubbersty Fold (like 'booth', 'fold' means a cowhouse or animal pen). Amongst the farms are Sharples Farm and Holmes Farm. Mellor Brook is the nearest village of any size in this well-wooded area.

◀ **BILSBORROW**
The White Bull c1955
B743005

Bilsborrow lies between Lancaster and Preston on the traffic-laden A6 road. The White Bull inn dates from the 18th century, and still believes in a roaring coal or log fire in winter. What used to be the turnpike road running from London to Scotland had a busy toll house, which is now the Green Man inn.

BILSBORROW
The Vicarage c1955
B743017

The vicarage in its spacious garden was built at about the same time as St Hilda's church, which was consecrated in 1927. Its peal of eight bells is well-known to campanologists. Money was left for the building of the stone church and tower in the will of Jane Salisbury, tragically killed on the railway in 1922. She was owner of Myerscough Hall. Bilsborrow is linked with the parishes of Myerscough and Barton, also lovely leafy areas.

BILSBORROW, *The Roebuck Hotel c1960* B743029

The old part of the Roebuck Hotel lies to the left of the buildings. Parish boundaries cross and re-cross with those of Myerscough and Barton - one boundary cuts through the bowling green of the Roebuck Inn, as it was known in earlier days. The Lancaster canal runs nearby, dug out by navvies in 1797. Tom Rowe, the Lancashire cheese factor, lived at York House in Bilsborrow.

BROUGHTON
The School c1965
B718008

Endowed in the 16th century, the free Broughton Grammar School also took children from Barton and Haighton. In the mid 19th century 80 pupils attended; Mr Alexander Jackson, a strict disciplinarian, held sway. A new school of stone was built opposite the old church about 50 years later.

BROUGHTON, *Woodplumpton Lane c1965* B718013

Woodplumpton is recorded in the Domesday Book. The fine modern houses are a world away from the ancient stocks outside Broughton churchyard, 18th-century Toll Bar Cottage, Pinfold Cottage or the smithy where the Mercer family used to shoe horses. Its popularity as a dormitory town near Preston to the north has brought heavy traffic.

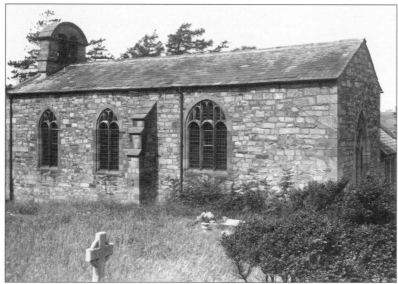

◀ **CLAUGHTON**
The Church c1955 C485003

The church of St Chad, with two bells hanging in its open belfry, stands a short distance down the lane opposite the Fenwick Arms. The larger bell on the right dated 1296 is the oldest dated bell in England. At the time of this photograph, Miss Rogers lived in the old rectory and grazed her goats in the churchyard. She reported: 'Last year the bell was brought down for repairs and I did what I never thought I could do in my life - I touched it!' In the church gable is the coat of arms of the ancient Croft family, whose graves are to be found in the churchyard. Also in the churchyard is the massive base of the medieval cross, which disappeared long ago.

◀ **CLAUGHTON**
The Fenwick Arms c1955
C485001

The hanging sign reads 'Café and Parking Ground'; this hostelry is on the way to Garstang. Alongside this inn was an old stone house dated 1705, which became the Parish Room in 1955. The Fenwicks, an influential family, had lived there - hence the inn's name. Claughton Hall, a Tudor mansion near the church, was moved stone by stone higher up into the hills.

▲ **CLAUGHTON,** *General View c1955* C485005

Claughton (pronounced 'Clafton') is situated three miles from Garstang; it is famed for herons, for there are twenty nests here. The old Claughton Garage and the Fenwick Arms can be seen in this view. The garage, owned by Nicholas Bamber, was later used by Mr R Seater for making hen cabins, which were in demand all over the Fylde. Realising that the mooted Garstang by pass would lose him trade, Mr Bamber bought a site on the A6 road and built a new garage. The by-pass was constructed by Messrs Lindsay Parkinson of Blackpool, who employed Irish labourers. Bowman Cottage, once a cobbler's thatched shop on the Fitzherbert-Brockholes estate, fell into dereliction along with other similar cottages.

◀ **LONGTON**
The Catholic Church c1960
L351002

This is the old St Oswald's Catholic church, which was replaced by a new one in 1965. Father O'Sullivan is the present incumbent. The parish dates from 1895, when Longton was a small village straggling along the Liverpool Road. Now very popular because of its proximity to Preston, Longton has burgeoned into a dormitory town with its own medical centre and library. The old Catholic church became a social center; in the early days, it was both church and school.

LONGTON
The Parish Church c1960
L351003

When the Anglo-Saxons settled in their village of 'Longetuna', meaning 'long village', it was cut off from the world by bogs and marshland. By the 17th century most villagers were involved in agriculture, along with allied trades like blacksmithing, wheelwrighting, and nail making. Carpet making, brewing ale and basket making followed. The church of St Andrew, Gothic in style, was built in 1887 to replace one built in 1773; a planned tower never materialised.

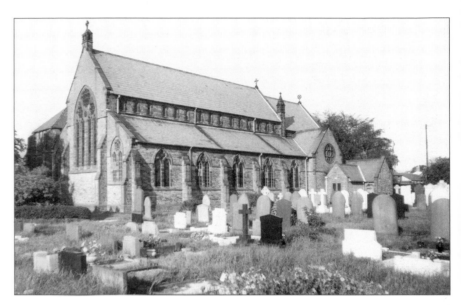

OVER KELLETT, *The Green c1955* O88004

Beside this part of the village green we see a grocer and newsagent's shop by the signpost pointing to Carnforth in one direction, Longridge in the other. The shop is an old property, and so is the long barn (left) under the trees, but some newer houses have appeared. This is limestone country, and there are underground streams and caves hereabouts.

OVERTON
The Church c1955
O121004

This church may have the oldest foundations of any in Lancashire, dating from Saxon times. Norman traces remain in the rounded doorway (right) with its massive oak door. Overton is situated near the Lune Estuary; it is said that a terrace on the main village street uses stone that came from Cockersand Abbey. Of the abbey, only the chapterhouse remains. The Ship Hotel has a case of 3,505 birds' eggs collected in the past by an enthusiastic landlord.

COWAN BRIDGE, *The Village c1955* C601001

Cowan Bridge lies two miles from Kirkby Lonsdale. Charlotte Bronte and her sisters spent such a spartan childhood at the school for clergymen's daughters here that she immortalised it in her famous novel 'Jane Eyre': 'We set out cold, arrived at church colder and during service became almost paralysed'. The Rev Carus Wilson, vicar of Tunstall, established the school in 1823. A commemorative tablet is on the wall of Bronte Cottage, the first house on the right next to the old road bridge.

COWAN BRIDGE
The Golden Cocker Café c1955 C601002

Here we have a closer view of the quiet main street; note the sign of the Golden Cocker Café by the street lamp. Petrol pumps and the small village shop stand next to another café advertising cigarettes and the ubiquitous Wall's ice cream. The signpost points to Casterton. Cowan Bridge is a place of pilgrimage for the Bronte Society. After the death of Maria and Elizabeth Bronte from typhus fever, the Rev Patrick Bronte removed his other daughters from Cowan Bridge School.

OVER KELLETT
The Village 1923 74160

On the village green, the memorial is mounted on to the pedestal of an old cross. The church of St Cuthbert is dedicated to that saint as he is thought to have stayed in the hamlet. It has a 14th-century tower, but most of St Cuthbert's dates from c1860. A charming tradition calls the children to sing from the top of the tower at Easter. Hall Garth, built c1800, stands opposite the cross; behind is a long stone barn to store corn.

STACKSTEADS, *Piper Bank c1955* S552003

Piper Bank appears in the census returns of 1851 and on maps of Rossendale as a place name. Edgeside Estate developed over and around it, sad to say swallowing up a horse trough which was fed from a spring in the hills and was thus never empty. Piper Road, like Booth Road where my mother was born, was an old toll road. Piper Bank, sweeping up towards the moors, is traversed by the road built in 1818 through the Glen. Glen Top Brewery (Baxter's) was rebuilt in 1894 with a new chimney, 'Old Smokey', the tallest in Rossendale. The area locally known as Thrutch Gorge features the long tunnel of the Rawtenstall to Bury railway, built in 1852. Road, river and rail run within twenty yards of Thrutch (a dialect Lancashire word synonymous with great effort). On 25 August 1902 an eighty-ton boiler crashed through waste ground at the Waterfoot end of Thrutch Gorge.

STACKSTEADS, *Fearns Hall c1955* S552002

Slater's Directory of 1876 lists this lovely Tudor mansion as Ferns Hall; it was supposed to date from 1557, but the earliest visible datestone over the porch is of 1696. The inscription above the door reads 'George Ashworth Cobham, great-grandson of George and Susanah Ashworth de Fearns and Catherine his wife ended this wing in the year 1830 on the site of that part of the old Mansion House which was built in the year 1557'. The mansion contained sixteen rooms and cellars, and nine bells for summoning servants hung near the kitchen. Later it became Fearns Hall Farmhouse, and later still it was divided into two residences. It was renovated in 1975.

THATCHED COTTAGES AND THE SEA

IN 1760 a law was passed outlawing chimney firing, which was what people did to clear away soot. Off the coast and in port, the sparks were a hazard to wooden ships and windmills - Cockerham Mill was burned down twice. Farms and cottages went up in smoke too if sparks were caught in thatched roofs. 'Houses supported on crooks (crucks)' were described in 1847 thus: 'A small porch led to a dark, low area open to smoky rafters. Bacon flitches and sides of beef hung above a large open fireplace'. The fire never went out.

Ben Alty was a turf man who cut fuel from Pilling Moss and brought peat turves to the villages on a pony cart. On some nights a cauldron of mixed oils and fat used to make seaboots waterproof bubbled away, making an aroma to challenge Chanel! How truly ancient the thatched dwellings were is instanced by Dudley Hall in Poulton-le-Fylde. The name is linked with Henry VIII's debt collectors Richard Empson and lawyer Dudley, who used this cottage when visiting in 1505. Their cruel impositions were never forgotten.

CHURCHTOWN, *The Parish Church c1955* C603005

The 12th-century church of St Helen was the parish church for Garstang, two miles away. Until they acquired their own church, Garstang villagers had to walk to Churchtown. This explains references in Bulmer's directory to 'the village of Garstang, Churchtown'. Henry IV had given oak beams for the roof in 1402. The church is full of treasures, not least the brass chandelier given by a builder following severe flooding from the River Wyre. An ancient pulpit, a Norman font and the gravestone of a medieval knight, besides old and interesting stones and graves in the churchyard, enthrall the visitor to this 'cathedral of the Fylde'. Restoration of the church by Mr Paley of Lancaster was completed in 1869. Traditional thatched cottages lined the cobbled streets leading to the church. Outside it stands an ancient slim pillar; some villagers call it the cross and others the sundial. Until the late 18th century, busy pot fairs were held around its base on the old market cross steps.

CHURCHTOWN
The Swing Bridge and the River Wyre c1955 C603006

The wooden swing bridge appeared on maps in 1847. Controversy arose between the different parishes when it was in need of repair, and Garstang Highways Board refused point blank to mend it in April 1885. Churchtown villagers used the bridge, which was situated near Catterall Hall. The last flood damage occurred in October 1980, when St Michael's village also suffered. A stronger bridge was officially opened by the vicar of Churchtown in 1984. The River Wyre flows into the Irish Sea at Fleetwood and rises near Tarnbrook in Wyresdale.

ST MICHAEL'S ON WYRE, *Garstang Road c1965* S551010

The Cherry Tree restaurant advertises its grills, well-known locally; from this point coach trips started, more ambitious in destination than the old wagonette trips. Road-side lamps have also changed in style, and traffic includes a heavy motor lorry (just visible in the distance) and a vintage invalid carriage (left). New bungalows pronounce the village's popularity as a place to retire or commute from, but the tolls charged by Shard Bridge Company to cross the river were a sore point.

▶ **ST MICHAEL'S ON WYRE**
The Cherry Tree Grill c1960
S551011

Note the old-style telephone box (left). Most of these cottages were built at the turn of the 19th century, when stops at Robinson's Tea Rooms were part of the popular wagonette trips. In those days the River Wyre had a good supply of salmon, which was usually on the menu at Robinson's. The members of St Michael's Sparrow Club were farmers backed by the Rural District Council; they made war on sparrows for damaging crops and building nests in thatch.

◀ **GREAT ECCLESTON**
Raikes Road c1965
G222073

To the left we can see G Hilton's confectioner's and grocer's shop. On the right is the post office, its thatched roof replaced by corrugated iron. Raikes Road had many thatched dwellings; as late as 1961, when alterations were afoot, one cottage proved to be a Fylde cruck-built cottage with clay and straw walls from the 16th century. In the distance are Bleasdale Fells.

▲ **GREAT ECCLESTON,** *The Square and West End c1960* G222004

We are close to Blackpool and Garstang. The old road curved through Little and Great Eccleston, but the by-pass of 1940 split these two villages. In 1823 William Bennet renewed his licence for the White Bull (right). He had to promise 'not to suffer any bear, bull or badger baiting, cock fighting nor permit any drinking or tippling during the hours of Divine Service'. Facing the White Bull was the Black Bull Inn. The Gala-Queen crowning is held annually here in the Square. Mentioned in Domesday Book, 'Eglestun' had a rush-bearing ceremony and a rush-light making industry. To celebrate Queen Victoria's coronation in 1837, all children were given oat cakes and beer. Celebrations nowadays merit no beer, but home-made ice-cream can be bought from the Willow Café, where two boys stand.

◄**GREAT ECCLESTON**
The Square c1965
G222060

Here we have another view of the White Bull Hotel, with Thomas, the grocer's, J N Kelley, and G L Owen the newsagent's nearby. A weekly farmers' market is held in the Square. The lamp replaced a cast iron lamp with a fluted pillar in 1936. In the 18th and early 19th century, houses were built on the edge of the square; the most famous dwelling in Great Eccleston is Leckonby Hall.

▼ **EUXTON,** *Runshaw Lane c1965* E207013

There was a village settlement here in the 13th century, and from time immemorial agriculture was the mainstay. In 1938, however, a large Royal Ordnance factory was opened, working day and night to supply munitions for World War II. In Dawber's Lane the craft of wattle and daub for cruck-built cottages was carried on, but Runshaw Lane has few signs of antiquity today.

► **COCKERHAM**
The Church c1960 C599004

A beam from the year of the Spanish Armada was found in the remains of the old church. The tall tower is all that remains of the 17th-century church, for the main part was rebuilt in the 19th century. Records show that one vicar buried eleven plague victims - he himself died from plague the next month. At St Michael's church one privilege the vicar had was to collect salmon from the baulk on the River Cocker on the first tide after the full moon. On the seashore at nearby Pilling ancient gravestones were found.

◀ **COCKERHAM**
Main Street c1960
C599005

On the right we can see a finger post pointing to the church. As the village was destroyed by fire in the 17th century, the village we see today was rebuilt after the fire some distance from the church. The sign on the gable end reads: 'The Parish Church of St Michael AD1134 The Revd D E F Ogden B A'.

▶ **COCKERHAM**
Main Street and the Post Office c1960
C599007

The village's name means 'a settlement by the River Cocker'. The village has rows of sandstone cottages and a number of farms. It was self-sufficient in the 19th century. There were two inns, the Manor and the Plough, where cock-fighting took place until it was outlawed. On Main Street were the blacksmith, the wheelwright, the fishmonger, the butcher and the post office, which was run by Mr R Ireland in his general stores (right).

COCKERHAM
The Old Rectory c1965
C599017

Besides a devastating fire, the original village of Cockerham also experienced flooding from the River Cocker, another reason to move to higher ground. On the site of the gardens of the Old Rectory was the windmill, which burned down in 1802 and yet again within 30 years. Called New Mill in 1840, it featured as a landmark on Captain Henry Mangles Denham's 'Instructions for approaching the new town and port of Fleetwood'.

FRECKLETON, *Lower Lane c1965* F197003

The rivers Ribble, Dow and Douglas meet at Freckleton, and were used by the Romans to get supplies to Kirkham. In 1725 the Quakers opened their burial ground in Lower Lane, planting a tree wherever one of their number was buried. A tragedy struck the village in August 1944 when an American bomber fell on the village school. The death toll was high.

FRECKLETON
Hallams c1965 F197010

Here in what was thought to be the largest village in the Fylde we have a good example of a Fylde cruck-built thatched homestead, of which very few remain. A corn mill flourished here from the 12th century until 1915, powered by water. Boat building was carried on, and sailcloth was made in cottages equipped with handlooms. Sailors and agricultural workers lived here, rope walks were busy, and so were the inns, the Plough and the Coach and Horses.

FRECKLETON, *The Village c1965* F197026

The war memorial stands on the triangular village green in the area within the railings, (far left). The Ship Inn up Bunker Street was the delight of smugglers in the 1770s, in the days when the toll road crossed Freckleton Moss. Grain, slate and coal were once brought to Freckleton Naze, and ocean-going ships were built at the shipyard, which was established in 1814, but the big event of the village now is Club Day in June.

GALGATE
The Boatyard c1960
G284013

The boatyard serves the marina, which has space for 100 boats. Lucas's boatbuilders are the premises near the large craft (centre). Popular regattas are held, and the Lancaster canal is nearby. Only just visible on the horizon is part of Lancaster University. The mainstay of Galgate villagers from 1790 to 1960 was the silk mill, where 400 people worked during the mill's heyday.

► **GALGATE**
The Bridge c1960
G284016

This fine stone bridge spans the Preston to Tewitfield Canal; alongside runs part of the A6 road. Railway trains travelling from London to Glasgow thunder nearby on a high viaduct. The plaque reading 'Number 86' alongside the arch possibly indicates this bridge's number – there are many bridges crossing the canal. Sedges and reed mace hide wading birds, coot and grebe, whilst swans and shelducks are not averse to sheltering under the bridge in stormy weather.

◄ **GALGATE**
Main Road c1960
G284020

The Green Dragon Hotel, a stone-built 18th-century inn, is popular with residents and students from Lancaster University. Facing the Green Dragon across the road is a terrace of stone cottages, with the New Inn at the end. Next door to the Green Dragon, an antiquated Regent petrol pump indicates a garage. Note the striped crossing marked by a Belisha beacon – these crossings were introduced around 1930.

▲ **HAMBLETON,** *The Creek c1960* H452019

This creek on the River Wyre near Poulton-le-Fylde has become part of a modern marina. The white building beyond the sailing boat (center left) is Wardley's Hotel. The three pointed gables to its left belong to the 1824 warehouses in which guano, flax and cotton were stored (it was pulled down in 1965). The ancient ports of Wardleys and Skippool near Hambleton Creek handled slaves and ships from Russia. 19th-century visitors to the creek came for 'Hambleton hookings', large mussels which sometimes contained a pearl.

◄ **HAMBLETON**
The Congregational Church and the Manse c1960 H452021

The land here on the corner of Paul's Lane and Sandy Lane was purchased for nine pounds in 1870. Founder members of Hambleton Congregational Church began building at once, carting the materials themselves. Amongst them were Edward Brewer, John Hodson, Thomas Eaves and the Thompson family. The church opened on 20 April 1870, and within 15 years a Sunday School was built. Ministers were supplied at first from the Fylde Itineracy. By 1970, when the church held its centenary, the Rev H C Oak Griffiths was the minister. The Manse (right) is now a private residence.

HEYSHAM
Stone Coffins 1891
28595

These six ancient graves hewn from solid rock close to the chapel of St Patrick lie on the impressive Heysham headland. St Patrick is said to have landed here after crossing the Irish Sea on a millstone. The chapel is one of the oldest in the country; the remains of its walls are 2ft 6ins thick, bonded with immensely strong mortar made by burning sea-shells – this method was used by the Romans.

▼ **HEYSHAM,** *The Village 1892* 30442

Quiet Heysham was once most famous for nettle beer and selling teas to trippers from its ancient cottages. The chapel on the headland and the stone coffins remain, but the ambience has changed. In 1904, two thousand workmen began digging a deep water harbour which took an army of Irish navvies seven years to complete. Heysham, once connected with Druids, has now become an important terminal for Irish sea traffic.

► **INSKIP**
Main Road c1950 164003

On the left we can see a line of old-fashioned telegraph poles. Not all post offices in the Fylde had a telegraph office early in the 20th century, nor could they deal with postal orders. Charles Ashton from Thornton-le-Fylde post office had to walk from there to Inskip on most days, and in snow he followed the telegraph poles. The tall chimney above the thatched cottage belonged to Tom Rowe's cheese factory. Run from Preston, it started business in 1930. Part of its sign can be seen just behind the vintage car.

◄ INSKIP
Main Road c1950
I64007

Winding, hedge-bound lanes and low-built cottages thatched with wheat straw were typical of Inskip, Treales, Wharles and other Fylde villages. When thatch had to be replaced with corrugated iron, it was not unusual to find hidden objects: swords from Cromwellian days, chalices, contraband and coins, or precious items from shipwrecks. Some hovels became uninhabitable because rats or birds infested the thatch.

KNOTT-END-ON-SEA
The Village c1960
K128043

An idea to rename this village St Bernard's-on-Sea in 1893 failed. The villagers would not accept it, although it was a valiant attempt to turn this Over-Wyre village into a popular watering place. To the right is Fleetwood Co-operative Society Ltd's grocery store. The road leads to the sea and the ferry service to Fleetwood across the River Wyre.

KNOTT-END-ON-SEA
The Ferry c1960
K128075

Fleetwood Urban District Council started the ferry service in 1894 with two sailing boats. The council bought the boats from the Croft family of Knott End, who had ferried villagers across the River Wyre for generations. This is a typical scene in the height of summer, when boats were crossing every few minutes. In the background we can see the tall Pharos lighthouse and the North Euston Hotel, designed in 1840 by the famous architect Sir Decimus Burton. In the foreground is the 'Lune Vale', one of the well-known ferry boats. Others were the 'Onward', the 'Bourne May', the 'Wyresdale' and the 'Progress'.

PILLING
Main Street c1960
P270008

The two ladies on the left are standing outside Pratt's shop, which according to its signs sells Lyons tea and cigarettes. Across the street is a café. Cyclists are approaching – there were many here, for the flat Fylde plain was ideal for cycling. The large sign opposite, although it is illegible, probably indicates Pilling Pottery. Birdwatchers delight in the surrounding mossland: in the 19th century, Gull Island was so clustered with nests that it was impossible to walk amongst them. Strangely enough, it was owned by a gentleman called Bird.

▼ **PILLING,** *The Old Ship Hotel c1955* P270001

This 18th-century inn was associated with smuggling - this isolated part of the coast was notorious for the illegal trade. Under cover of darkness, brandy, tobacco and bolts of lace and velvet were brought along Velvet Lane from the shore. A typical tavern on Pilling Moss, the Old Ship still has a pump in the yard embossed with the initials of the Nicholson family and dated 1782.The spire of St John's church can be seen in the background.

► **SILVERDALE**
The Road to the Beach c1955 S609003

Silverdale is a beautiful limestone village in the midst of woods and craggy outcrops. It is classed an Area of Outstanding Natural Beauty, and has always attracted visitors, some of them famous, like Mrs Elizabeth Gaskell with her 19th-century awareness of struggling workers. She married a Manchester Unitarian minister in 1832 and stayed at Lindeth Tower (dated 1816) in Silverdale. From here she described the sunsets and the views across the Kent estuary and the Irish Sea.

◀ **SILVERDALE**
Emesgate Lane
c1955 S609044

T A Wilkinson the chemist is next door to the shop selling Wall's ice cream with rustic furniture outside. The village gets its name from a Viking, Sigward. There is a record of a chapel here in about 1050, situated where Cove Lane meets Emesgate Lane. The church of St John replaced it; the old gravestones were transferred to the new site, and they yield interesting information.

▶ **SILVERDALE**
Old Cottages near the Beach, Cove Lane c1955
S609047

On Cove Lane there was an ancient chapel. The lane also led to Jenny Brown's Point, where an old lady of that name lived in the 18th century. Copper smelting was carried on here, and the chimney stack at Crag Foot became a useful landmark for travellers crossing the dangerous sands of Morecambe Bay. In the 1920s Silverdale village was left high and dry, for the River Kent changed course. Before that steamers called here.

SINGLETON, *The Post Office c1960* S692005

Outside Holroyd's shop and post office is a sign warning of a low bridge ahead. Opposite this leafy corner was the vicarage, now a private house. This pleasant Fylde village was rebuilt by Thomas Horrocks Miller. He succeeded Alderman Thomas Miller as lord of the manor in 1865, and lived at Singleton Park. He had a great interest in land drainage, and he owned valuable antiques. He also owned a famous stallion, Honest Tom, which died in 1885. Squire Miller had the horse's head preserved.

STAINING
Thornfield Holiday Camp c1955 S694008

We can see the 19th-century church of St Luke in the background amidst the trees. The village became Increasingly popular with visitors because of its proximity to Blackpool, but caravans and a holiday camp seem at odds with a village recorded in the Domesday Book. In Mill Lane is one of the Fylde's old windmills for grinding local corn. Like those at Kirkham, Wrea Green and Preesall, it is now a private residence.

SLYNE, *Post Office Corner c1955* S555003

The post office is on the far left, and immediately next door is A Shenton, dealing in baby linen and ladies' clothes. Taylors (centre) have a double-fronted shop, a sign that electrical goods and electricians are increasingly in demand. There is a recreation ground (right) and some motor traffic. Slyne, with Hest, also near Lancaster, saw Bonnie Prince Charlie's 1845 army of Scots passing on their way south. Hest Bank remains the starting point for Guide Cedric Robinson to lead groups safely across the treacherous quicksands of Morecambe Bay.

TARLETON
St Mary's Church
c1955 T199002

Few people think of
Tarleton as a port, but in the
15th century ships from
here sailed to small ports
along the Lancashire coast
and even to Europe. Built in
1717, St Mary's was
troubled with flooding from
the River Douglas, and Holy
Trinity church, consecrated
in 1888, is more centrally
convenient. Antiquity
shows in the datestone
(1660) of the Ram's Head, a
coaching inn on the
Ormskirk to Preston road.
Tarleton's mossland was
drained in order to produce
crops. At Tarleton Lock the
river Douglas meets the
Leeds and Liverpool Canal.
Harry Mayor was lock
keeper here for forty-seven
years.

THORNTON-CLEVELEYS
Victoria Road East c1960
T307020

The parade of shops (left) proclaims that a once quiet seaside village is becoming a busy township - we can see Ellwood's, the Midland Bank, a chemist, and a newsagent and tobacconist. Regular bus services came about rapidly; Victoria Road was the main route. It was once known as Ramper, a high dyke built (along with the draining of Thornton Marsh) to keep back the sea. The eastern end of the road leads to the restored Marsh windmill and its village complex, which was opened by the Duke of Westminster.

WREA GREEN
The Duck Pond c1965
W527014

This is perhaps the largest
village green in Lancashire,
although the duck pond
seems to be diminishing.
Cottages, the Grapes Inn,
the church and the school
are facing or clustered
round the green. An old
resident, Mrs Lancaster, had
a fund of memories. She
was a Rose Queen one Club
Day. She recalled Pudding
Pie Nook, thatched cottages
knocked down and replaced
by bungalows. In 1910 Mr
Tod Hull was the oldest
resident. Lovers' Lane was
glorious with bluebells and
wood anemones in spring.

WREA GREEN, *The School c1965* W527018

There has been a school here for 300 years. In the 17th century James Thistleton left money for building a Free School, and in the 18th century Nicholas Sharples from London gave money to it because he remembered his childhood in the village. Miss Croft and Mrs Cardwell taught at the school in the 1920s. Village characters once abounded; one of them was Cockle Maggie, who like Molly Malone from Ireland worked the village selling Lytham shellfish and freshly-caught eels. In 1959 Wrea Green won Lancashire's Best Kept Village competition.

INDEX

Aughton 46-47

Balderstone 73

Barley 17

Barrowford 16

Bashall Eaves 32-33, 59

Bilsborrow 73, 74

Blacko 18

Bolton-by-Rowland 23, 24-25

Brookhouse 46

Broughton 75

Caton 44, 45

Chatburn 18, 19, 20-21

Chipping 33, 34

Churchtown 84, 85

Claughton 76, 77

Cockerham 88-89, 90

Cowan Bridge 79, 80-81

Croston 70, 71

Dolphinholme 34-35, 36

Downham 21, 22

Dunsop Bridge 26, 58, 59

Euxton 88

Freckleton 90, 91

Galgate 92-93, 94-95

Gisburn 25, 60-61

Great Eccleston 86, 87

Great Mitton 64, 65

Grindleton 27, 30-31

Halton 65, 66-67

Hambleton 95

Heysham 96-97, 98

Hoghton 72-73

Hornby 67, 68-69, 70

Hurst Green 37, 38

Inskip 98-99

Knott-End-on-Sea 99, 100-101

Langho 28-29

Longton 77, 78

Newchurch In Pendle 28, 29

Newton 62-63

Newton-in-Bowland 64

Old Langho 60

Over Kellett 78, 82

Overton 79

Pendleton 38-39

Pilling 102-103, 104

Pleasington 50

Ribchester 51, 52-53, 54

Rimington 39

Rivington 40-41

Rufford 54

Sabden 55, 56-57

St Michael's on Wyre 85, 86-87

Sawley Abbey 47, 48-49

Silverdale 104-105

Singleton 106

Slaidburn 40, 41, 61

Slyne 107

Stacksteads 82, 83

Staining 107

Tarleton 108-109

Thornton-Cleveleys 110-111

Waddington 41, 42, 43

Warton 43, 44

Wray 50-51

Wrea Green 112-113, 114

Frith Book Co Titles

www.francisfrith.co.uk

The Frith Book Company publishes over 100 new titles each year. A selection of those currently available are listed below. For latest catalogue please contact Frith Book Co.

Town Books 96 pages, approximately 100 photos. **County and Themed Books** 128 pages, approximately 150 photos (unless specified). All titles hardback with laminated case and jacket, except those indicated pb (paperback)

Amersham, Chesham & Rickmansworth (pb)	1-85937-340-2	£9.99	Devon (pb)	1-85937-297-x	£9.99
Andover (pb)	1-85937-292-9	£9.99	Devon Churches (pb)	1-85937-250-3	£9.99
Aylesbury (pb)	1-85937-227-9	£9.99	Dorchester (pb)	1-85937-307-0	£9.99
Barnstaple (pb)	1-85937-300-3	£9.99	Dorset (pb)	1-85937-269-4	£9.99
Basildon Living Memories (pb)	1-85937-515-4	£9.99	Dorset Coast (pb)	1-85937-299-6	£9.99
Bath (pb)	1-85937-419-0	£9.99	Dorset Living Memories (pb)	1-85937-584-7	£9.99
Bedford (pb)	1-85937-205-8	£9.99	Down the Severn (pb)	1-85937-560-x	£9.99
Bedfordshire Living Memories	1-85937-513-8	£14.99	Down The Thames (pb)	1-85937-278-3	£9.99
Belfast (pb)	1-85937-303-8	£9.99	Down the Trent	1-85937-311-9	£14.99
Berkshire (pb)	1-85937-191-4	£9.99	East Anglia (pb)	1-85937-265-1	£9.99
Berkshire Churches	1-85937-170-1	£17.99	East Grinstead (pb)	1-85937-138-8	£9.99
Berkshire Living Memories	1-85937-332-1	£14.99	East London	1-85937-080-2	£14.99
Black Country	1-85937-497-2	£12.99	East Sussex (pb)	1-85937-606-1	£9.99
Blackpool (pb)	1-85937-393-3	£9.99	Eastbourne (pb)	1-85937-399-2	£9.99
Bognor Regis (pb)	1-85937-431-x	£9.99	Edinburgh (pb)	1-85937-193-0	£8.99
Bournemouth (pb)	1-85937-545-6	£9.99	England In The 1880s	1-85937-331-3	£17.99
Bradford (pb)	1-85937-204-x	£9.99	Essex - Second Selection	1-85937-456-5	£14.99
Bridgend (pb)	1-85937-386-0	£7.99	Essex (pb)	1-85937-270-8	£9.99
Bridgwater (pb)	1-85937-305-4	£9.99	Essex Coast	1-85937-342-9	£14.99
Bridport (pb)	1-85937-327-5	£9.99	Essex Living Memories	1-85937-490-5	£14.99
Brighton (pb)	1-85937-192-2	£8.99	Exeter	1-85937-539-1	£9.99
Bristol (pb)	1-85937-264-3	£9.99	Exmoor (pb)	1-85937-608-8	£9.99
British Life A Century Ago (pb)	1-85937-213-9	£9.99	Falmouth (pb)	1-85937-594-4	£9.99
Buckinghamshire (pb)	1-85937-200-7	£9.99	Folkestone (pb)	1-85937-124-8	£9.99
Camberley (pb)	1-85937-222-8	£9.99	Frome (pb)	1-85937-317-8	£9.99
Cambridge (pb)	1-85937-422-0	£9.99	Glamorgan	1-85937-488-3	£14.99
Cambridgeshire (pb)	1-85937-420-4	£9.99	Glasgow (pb)	1-85937-190-6	£9.99
Cambridgeshire Villages	1-85937-523-5	£14.99	Glastonbury (pb)	1-85937-338-0	£7.99
Canals And Waterways (pb)	1-85937-291-0	£9.99	Gloucester (pb)	1-85937-232-5	£9.99
Canterbury Cathedral (pb)	1-85937-179-5	£9.99	Gloucestershire (pb)	1-85937-561-8	£9.99
Cardiff (pb)	1-85937-093-4	£9.99	Great Yarmouth (pb)	1-85937-426-3	£9.99
Carmarthenshire (pb)	1-85937-604-5	£9.99	Greater Manchester (pb)	1-85937-266-x	£9.99
Chelmsford (pb)	1-85937-310-0	£9.99	Guildford (pb)	1-85937-410-7	£9.99
Cheltenham (pb)	1-85937-095-0	£9.99	Hampshire (pb)	1-85937-279-1	£9.99
Cheshire (pb)	1-85937-271-6	£9.99	Harrogate (pb)	1-85937-423-9	£9.99
Chester (pb)	1-85937-382 8	£9.99	Hastings and Bexhill (pb)	1-85937-131-0	£9.99
Chesterfield (pb)	1-85937-378-x	£9.99	Heart of Lancashire (pb)	1-85937-197-3	£9.99
Chichester (pb)	1-85937-228-7	£9.99	Helston (pb)	1-85937-214-7	£9.99
Churches of East Cornwall (pb)	1-85937-249-x	£9.99	Hereford (pb)	1-85937-175-2	£9.99
Churches of Hampshire (pb)	1-85937-207-4	£9.99	Herefordshire (pb)	1-85937-567-7	£9.99
Cinque Ports & Two Ancient Towns	1-85937-492-1	£14.99	Herefordshire Living Memories	1-85937-514-6	£14.99
Colchester (pb)	1-85937-188-4	£8.99	Hertfordshire (pb)	1-85937-247-3	£9.99
Cornwall (pb)	1-85937-229-5	£9.99	Horsham (pb)	1-85937-432-8	£9.99
Cornwall Living Memories	1-85937-248-1	£14.99	Humberside (pb)	1-85937-605-3	£9.99
Cotswolds (pb)	1-85937-230-9	£9.99	Hythe, Romney Marsh, Ashford (pb)	1-85937-256-2	£9.99
Cotswolds Living Memories	1-85937-255-4	£14.99	Ipswich (pb)	1-85937-424-7	£9.99
County Durham (pb)	1-85937-398-4	£9.99	Isle of Man (pb)	1-85937-268-6	£9.99
Croydon Living Memories (pb)	1-85937-162-0	£9.99	Isle of Wight (pb)	1-85937-429-8	£9.99
Cumbria (pb)	1-85937-621-5	£9.99	Isle of Wight Living Memories	1-85937-304-6	£14.99
Derby (pb)	1-85937-367-4	£9.99	Kent (pb)	1-85937-189-2	£9.99
Derbyshire (pb)	1-85937-196-5	£9.99	Kent Living Memories(pb)	1-85937-401-8	£9.99
Derbyshire Living Memories	1-85937-330-5	£14.99	Kings Lynn (pb)	1-85937-334-8	£9.99

Available from your local bookshop or from the publisher

Frith Book Co Titles (continued)

Title	ISBN	Price	Title	ISBN	Price
Lake District (pb)	1-85937-275-9	£9.99	Sherborne (pb)	1-85937-301-1	£9.99
Lancashire Living Memories	1-85937-335-6	£14.99	Shrewsbury (pb)	1-85937-325-9	£9.99
Lancaster, Morecambe, Heysham (pb)	1-85937-233-3	£9.99	Shropshire (pb)	1-85937-326-7	£9.99
Leeds (pb)	1-85937-202-3	£9.99	Shropshire Living Memories	1-85937-643-6	£14.99
Leicester (pb)	1-85937-381-x	£9.99	Somerset	1-85937-153-1	£14.99
Leicestershire & Rutland Living Memories	1-85937-500-6	£12.99	South Devon Coast	1-85937-107-8	£14.99
Leicestershire (pb)	1-85937-185-x	£9.99	South Devon Living Memories (pb)	1-85937-609-6	£9.99
Lighthouses	1-85937-257-0	£9.99	South East London (pb)	1-85937-263-5	£9.99
Lincoln (pb)	1-85937-380-1	£9.99	South Somerset	1-85937-318-6	£14.99
Lincolnshire (pb)	1-85937-433-6	£9.99	South Wales	1-85937-519-7	£14.99
Liverpool and Merseyside (pb)	1-85937-234-1	£9.99	Southampton (pb)	1-85937-427-1	£9.99
London (pb)	1-85937-183-3	£9.99	Southend (pb)	1-85937-313-5	£9.99
London Living Memories	1-85937-454-9	£14.99	Southport (pb)	1-85937-425-5	£9.99
Ludlow (pb)	1-85937-176-0	£9.99	St Albans (pb)	1-85937-341-0	£9.99
Luton (pb)	1-85937-235-x	£9.99	St Ives (pb)	1-85937-415-8	£9.99
Maidenhead (pb)	1-85937-339-9	£9.99	Stafford Living Memories (pb)	1-85937-503-0	£9.99
Maidstone (pb)	1-85937-391-7	£9.99	Staffordshire (pb)	1-85937-308-9	£9.99
Manchester (pb)	1-85937-198-1	£9.99	Stourbridge (pb)	1-85937-530-8	£9.99
Marlborough (pb)	1-85937-336-4	£9.99	Stratford upon Avon (pb)	1-85937-388-7	£9.99
Middlesex	1-85937-158-2	£14.99	Suffolk (pb)	1-85937-221-x	£9.99
Monmouthshire	1-85937-532-4	£14.99	Suffolk Coast (pb)	1-85937-610-x	£9.99
New Forest (pb)	1-85937-390-9	£9.99	Surrey (pb)	1-85937-240-6	£9.99
Newark (pb)	1-85937-366-6	£9.99	Surrey Living Memories	1-85937-328-3	£14.99
Newport, Wales (pb)	1-85937-258-9	£9.99	Sussex (pb)	1-85937-184-1	£9.99
Newquay (pb)	1-85937-421-2	£9.99	Sutton (pb)	1-85937-337-2	£9.99
Norfolk (pb)	1-85937-195-7	£9.99	Swansea (pb)	1-85937-167-1	£9.99
Norfolk Broads	1-85937-486-7	£14.99	Taunton (pb)	1-85937-314-3	£9.99
Norfolk Living Memories (pb)	1-85937-402-6	£9.99	Tees Valley & Cleveland (pb)	1-85937-623-1	£9.99
North Buckinghamshire	1-85937-626-6	£14.99	Teignmouth (pb)	1-85937-370-4	£7.99
North Devon Living Memories	1-85937-261-9	£14.99	Thanet (pb)	1-85937-116-7	£9.99
North Hertfordshire	1-85937-547-2	£14.99	Tiverton (pb)	1-85937-178-7	£9.99
North London (pb)	1-85937-403-4	£9.99	Torbay (pb)	1-85937-597-9	£9.99
North Somerset	1-85937-302-x	£14.99	Truro (pb)	1-85937-598-7	£9.99
North Wales (pb)	1-85937-298-8	£9.99	Victorian & Edwardian Dorset	1-85937-254-6	£14.99
North Yorkshire (pb)	1-85937-236-8	£9.99	Victorian & Edwardian Kent (pb)	1-85937-624-X	£9.99
Northamptonshire Living Memories	1-85937-529-4	£14.99	Victorian & Edwardian Maritime Album (pb)	1-85937-622-3	£9.99
Northamptonshire	1-85937-150-7	£14.99	Victorian and Edwardian Sussex (pb)	1-85937-625-8	£9.99
Northumberland Tyne & Wear (pb)	1-85937-281-3	£9.99	Villages of Devon (pb)	1-85937-293-7	£9.99
Northumberland	1-85937-522-7	£14.99	Villages of Kent (pb)	1-85937-294-5	£9.99
Norwich (pb)	1-85937-194-9	£8.99	Villages of Sussex (pb)	1-85937-295-3	£9.99
Nottingham (pb)	1-85937-324-0	£9.99	Warrington (pb)	1-85937-507-3	£9.99
Nottinghamshire (pb)	1-85937-187-6	£9.99	Warwick (pb)	1-85937-518-9	£9.99
Oxford (pb)	1-85937-411-5	£9.99	Warwickshire (pb)	1-85937-203-1	£9.99
Oxfordshire (pb)	1-85937-430-1	£9.99	Welsh Castles (pb)	1-85937-322-4	£9.99
Oxfordshire Living Memories	1-85937-525-1	£14.99	West Midlands (pb)	1-85937-289-9	£9.99
Paignton (pb)	1-85937-374-7	£7.99	West Sussex (pb)	1-85937-607-x	£9.99
Peak District (pb)	1-85937-280-5	£9.99	West Yorkshire (pb)	1-85937-201-5	£9.99
Pembrokeshire	1-85937-262-7	£14.99	Weston Super Mare (pb)	1-85937-306-2	£9.99
Penzance (pb)	1-85937-595-2	£9.99	Weymouth (pb)	1-85937-209-0	£9.99
Peterborough (pb)	1-85937-219-8	£9.99	Wiltshire (pb)	1-85937-277-5	£9.99
Picturesque Harbours	1-85937-208-2	£14.99	Wiltshire Churches (pb)	1-85937-171-x	£9.99
Piers	1-85937-237-6	£17.99	Wiltshire Living Memories (pb)	1-85937-396-8	£9.99
Plymouth (pb)	1-85937-389-5	£9.99	Winchester (pb)	1-85937-428-x	£9.99
Poole & Sandbanks (pb)	1-85937-251-1	£9.99	Windsor (pb)	1-85937-333-x	£9.99
Preston (pb)	1-85937-212-0	£9.99	Wokingham & Bracknell (pb)	1-85937-329-1	£9.99
Reading (pb)	1-85937-238-4	£9.99	Woodbridge (pb)	1-85937-498-0	£9.99
Redhill to Reigate (pb)	1-85937-596-0	£9.99	Worcester (pb)	1-85937-165-5	£9.99
Ringwood (pb)	1-85937-384-4	£7.99	Worcestershire Living Memories	1-85937-489-1	£14.99
Romford (pb)	1-85937-319-4	£9.99	Worcestershire	1-85937-152-3	£14.99
Royal Tunbridge Wells (pb)	1-85937-504-9	£9.99	York (pb)	1-85937-199-x	£9.99
Salisbury (pb)	1-85937-239-2	£9.99	Yorkshire (pb)	1-85937-186-8	£9.99
Scarborough (pb)	1-85937-379-8	£9.99	Yorkshire Coastal Memories	1-85937-506-5	£14.99
Sevenoaks and Tonbridge (pb)	1-85937-392-5	£9.99	Yorkshire Dales	1-85937-502-2	£14.99
Sheffield & South Yorks (pb)	1-85937-267-8	£9.99	Yorkshire Living Memories (pb)	1-85937-397-6	£9.99

See Frith books on the internet at www.francisfrith.co.uk

FRITH PRODUCTS & SERVICES

Francis Frith would doubtless be pleased to know that the pioneering publishing venture he started in 1860 still continues today. Over a hundred and forty years later, The Francis Frith Collection continues in the same innovative tradition and is now one of the foremost publishers of vintage photographs in the world. Some of the current activities include:

Interior Decoration

Today Frith's photographs can be seen framed and as giant wall murals in thousands of pubs, restaurants, hotels, banks, retail stores and other public buildings throughout the country. In every case they enhance the unique local atmosphere of the places they depict and provide reminders of gentler days in an increasingly busy and frenetic world.

Product Promotions

Frith products are used by many major companies to promote the sales of their own products or to reinforce their own history and heritage. Frith promotions have been used by Hovis bread, Courage beers, Scots Porage Oats, Colman's mustard, Cadbury's foods, Mellow Birds coffee, Dunhill pipe tobacco, Guinness, and Bulmer's Cider.

Genealogy and Family History

As the interest in family history and roots grows world-wide, more and more people are turning to Frith's photographs of Great Britain for images of the towns, villages and streets where their ancestors lived; and, of course, photographs of the churches and chapels where their ancestors were christened, married and buried are an essential part of every genealogy tree and family album.

Frith Products

All Frith photographs are available Framed or just as Mounted Prints and Posters (size 23 x 16 inches). These may be ordered from the address below. From time to time other products - Address Books, Calendars, Table Mats, etc - are available.

The Internet

Already fifty thousand Frith photographs can be viewed and purchased on the internet through the Frith websites and a myriad of partner sites.

For more detailed information on Frith companies and products, look at these sites:

www.francisfrith.co.uk
www.francisfrith.com
(for North American visitors)

See the complete list of Frith Books at:

www.francisfrith.co.uk

This web site is regularly updated with the latest list of publications from the Frith Book Company. If you wish to buy books relating to another part of the country that your local bookshop does not stock, you may purchase on-line.

For further information, trade, or author enquiries please contact us at the address below:
The Francis Frith Collection, Frith's Barn, Teffont, Salisbury, Wiltshire, England SP3 5QP.
Tel: +44 (0)1722 716 376 Fax: +44 (0)1722 716 881   Email: sales@francisfrith.co.uk

See Frith books on the internet at www.francisfrith.co.uk

FREE MOUNTED PRINT

Mounted Print
Overall size 14 x 11 inches

Fill in and cut out this voucher and return
it with your remittance for £2.25 (to cover postage and handling). Offer valid for delivery to UK addresses only.

Choose any photograph included in this book.
Your SEPIA print will be A4 in size. It will be mounted in a cream mount with a burgundy rule line (overall size 14 x 11 inches).

Order additional Mounted Prints at HALF PRICE (only £7.49 each*)
If you would like to order more Frith prints from this book, possibly as gifts for friends and family, you can buy them at half price (with no additional postage and handling costs).

Have your Mounted Prints framed
For an extra £14.95 per print* you can have your mounted print(s) framed in an elegant polished wood and gilt moulding, overall size 16 x 13 inches (no additional postage and handling required).

---

* IMPORTANT!

These special prices are only available if you order at the same time as you order your free mounted print. You must use the ORIGINAL VOUCHER on this page (no copies permitted). We can only despatch to one address.

Send completed Voucher form to:
The Francis Frith Collection, Frith's Barn, Teffont, Salisbury, Wiltshire SP3 5QP

CHOOSE ANY IMAGE FROM THIS BOOK

Voucher for **FREE** and Reduced Price Frith Prints

Please do not photocopy this voucher. Only the original is valid, so please fill it in, cut it out and return it to us with your order.

Picture ref no	Page no	Qty	Mounted @ £7.49	Framed + £14.95	Total Cost
		1	Free of charge*	£	£
			£7.49	£	£
			£7.49	£	£
			£7.49	£	£
			£7.49	£	£
			£7.49	£	£

Please allow 28 days for delivery

* Post & handling (UK)	£2.25
Total Order Cost	£

Title of this book . . . .

I enclose a cheque/postal order for £ . . . .
made payable to 'The Francis Frith Collection'

OR please debit my Mastercard / Visa / Switch / Amex card
(credit cards please on all overseas orders), details below

Card Number

Issue No (Switch only)   Valid from (Amex/Switch)

Expires   Signature

Name Mr/Mrs/Ms ....

Address ....

....

....

.... Postcode ....

Daytime Tel No ....

Email ....

Valid to 31/12/05

Free Print - see overleaf

Would you like to find out more about Francis Frith?

We have recently recruited some entertaining speakers who are happy to visit local groups, clubs and societies to give an illustrated talk documenting Frith's travels and photographs. If you are a member of such a group and are interested in hosting a presentation, we would love to hear from you.

Our speakers bring with them a small selection of our local town and county books, together with sample prints. They are happy to take orders. A small proportion of the order value is donated to the group who have hosted the presentation. The talks are therefore an excellent way of fundraising for small groups and societies.

Can you help us with information about any of the Frith photographs in this book?

We are gradually compiling an historical record for each of the photographs in the Frith archive. It is always fascinating to find out the names of the people shown in the pictures, as well as insights into the shops, buildings and other features depicted.

If you recognize anyone in the photographs in this book, or if you have information not already included in the author's caption, do let us know. We would love to hear from you, and will try to publish it in future books or articles.

Our production team

Frith books are produced by a small dedicated team at offices in the converted Grade II listed 18th-century barn at Teffont near Salisbury, illustrated above. Most have worked with the Frith Collection for many years. All have in common one quality: they have a passion for the Frith Collection. The team is constantly expanding, but currently includes:

Jason Buck, John Buck, Douglas Mitchell-Burns, Ruth Butler, Heather Crisp, Isobel Hall, Julian Hight, Peter Horne, James Kinnear, Karen Kinnear, Tina Leary, David Marsh, Sue Molloy, Kate Rotondetto, Dean Scource, Eliza Sackett, Terence Sackett, Sandra Sampson, Adrian Sanders, Sandra Sanger, Julia Skinner, Lewis Taylor, Shelley Tolcher and Lorraine Tuck.